C000193343

About this Learning Guide

Shmoop Will Make You a Better Lover*
*of Literature, History, Poetry, Life...

Our lively learning guides are written by experts and educators who want to show your brain a good time. Shmoop writers come primarily from Ph.D. programs at top universities, including Stanford, Harvard, and UC Berkeley.

Want more Shmoop? We cover literature, poetry, bestsellers, music, US history, civics, biographies (and the list keeps growing). Drop by our website to see the latest.

www.shmoop.com

Table of Contents

Introduction

In a Nutshell

Breakfast at Tiffany's is the story of a young woman in World War II-era New York who hobnobs with famous people, gets into a lot of trouble, and breaks many hearts along the way, all while struggling to find her place in the world. And it's one of Truman Capote's most famous works, due in large part to the film adaptation of it.

The novel was written in 1958, and in 1961 the film version starring Audrey Hepburn was released. It was her portrayal of Holly Golightly that made the film a hit, and Hepburn's dark glasses and little black dress soon became fashion icons. The film also featured a soundtrack by musician Henry Mancini, and "Moon River," the song he created for the movie's theme, won an Oscar and is considered a classic as well.

Though the novel itself sometimes gets lost in discussions of the film, it was and is considered pretty remarkable in its own right. Upon its publication, Norman Mailer, a well-respected American writer, is quoted as saying that he "would not have changed two words in *Breakfast at Tiffany's* , which will become a small classic." And, according to Capote's biographer Gerald Clarke, Holly Golightly became Capote's favorite character of all the ones he created (some say this is because Holly resembles Capote). His success with capturing the subject of this book could be because Capote inhabited the same type of world that Holly does and because, as Clarke explained in the biography, Capote based his favorite character on a number of real-life women he knew (including Chaplin's wife Oona and Gloria Vanderbilt). Either way, the short novel created a lot of buzz among critics and in Capote's own social circle, so this makes the book a pretty interesting blend of literary achievement and pop culture text.

Why Should I Care?

When it comes down to it, Holly Golightly is trying to find herself (we know this is a terrible cliché, but we think it's pretty true in this case). Holly is nineteen years old and she's trying to figure out who she is, what she wants in her life, what her place in the world is, and what will make her happy. And aren't these some things we can all relate to, especially as we try to navigate the messy business of being in high school and college?

Although the specific experiences of Holly's life might not mirror our own, the struggles she goes through and the heavy questions she deals with probably do reflect many of the things any of us face every day. We might not visit mobsters in prison or run off to South America at the drop of a hat (while evading police, no less), but we probably do know what it's like to wrestle with our self-identity and to try to find a place where we feel comfortable and settled. And this can seem as difficult for us at times as it does for Holly. Because, if we look a little deeper, it sure can speak to our own experiences. Because there might be a little bit of Holly Golightly in all of us.

Summary

Book Summary

The novel opens in New York during World War II. We're introduced to an unnamed narrator who moves into a brownstone apartment building in the city in order pursue his career as a writer. Shortly after moving into the apartment, he sees Holiday Golightly (she goes by Holly for most of the novel) for the first time late one night in the hall of the apartment building, but it takes a while before he actually meets her face-to-face.

And then one night his life changes entirely when Holly knocks on his bedroom window after she's been sitting out on the fire escape watching him. He lets her in and after the two get to know each other a little better, Holly crawls into the narrator's bed (just so she can get some rest) because he reminds her of her brother Fred and she feels safe with him. But when she starts crying, and when the narrator asks her about it, Holly rushes back to her own apartment (and we and the narrator learn that Holly doesn't like discussing anything too personal about her life).

Holly and the narrator start to spend some time together, and he learns that Holly is in the habit of entertaining lots of different men at loud parties in her apartment. He's invited to one of these parties and, among others, meets a Hollywood agent named O.J. Berman, who once tried to get Holly into movies, and a man named Rusty Trawler, who pretends he loves Holly but who she thinks is actually gay. The narrator also meets Mag Wildwood at one of these soirees (she's a model who can't hold her liquor and who Holly doesn't like very much). Mag is engaged to a Brazilian diplomat named José Ybarra-Jaegar (he becomes important to the story a little later on).

One of the ways Holly earns money is by visiting alleged mobster Sally Tomato in prison every week. The visits seem innocent enough, and Holly gets paid to send weather reports back to Sally's lawyer (whose name is O'Shaughnessy). But we soon learn that these weather reports aren't as innocent as they seem.

At some point, Holly, Rusty, Mag, and José take a trip to Florida, and after Mag and Rusty both end up in the hospital, Holly and José start an affair with each other that ends up with Holly getting pregnant. Mag and Rusty find out about the affair and marry each other instead (the marriage ends badly, we later learn). Does this sound enough like a soap opera yet? Wait, there's more!

José eventually proposes to Holly and she makes plans to move to Brazil to be with him. This devastates the narrator, who has fallen a little in love with Holly and who has come to depend on having her in his life. But he agrees to go horseback riding with her in Central Park a few days before she's scheduled to leave New York so she can say good-bye to her favorite horse. The ride is a disaster in more ways than one. The narrator's horse freaks out and takes off with the narrator still on him. So Holly rides hard to catch up to the narrator and to save him, an overexertion that causes her to lose the baby (though we don't know that yet).

Later the same evening, Holly is tending to the narrator, who is still sore and battered from the horseback ride, when she's confronted by two detectives who arrest her for being part of a drug ring headed by Sally Tomato. It seems those weather reports were actually messages about drug shipments (which Holly is unaware of), and she's taken into custody and her name is splashed all over the evening newspapers. José loves Holly, but he decides that he can't risk being associated with any scandal since it could ruin his political career. He writes her a "Dear John" letter and returns to Brazil without her (keep in mind that he thinks she is still pregnant with his child).

Since Holly no longer has married life with José to look forward to, she decides she's going to leave the country (even though she's still under investigation for the drug charges), and decides she's going to head to Brazil anyway since José has already paid for her ticket. She asks the narrator to help her gather her things since she's being watched by the authorities (which he does), and she eventually makes it to the airport and goes on her way.

A lot of time passes before the narrator hears from Holly, but he finally gets a postcard from her. It seems she's made her way to Buenos Aires where she's fallen in love with a rich (and married) man. She promises to write the narrator again once she has a permanent address, but we learn that he never hears from her again and he's left wondering what becomes of her and whether she ever finds happiness.

Chapter 1

- We are introduced to the narrator in this first chapter (who is nameless) and learn that he often returns to the places he's lived throughout his life. He recalls for us his "first New York apartment" (1.1), a rundown "brownstone in the East Seventies" (1.1) with old furniture and walls that are "a color rather like tobacco-spit" (1.1). Sounds charming, doesn't it?
- The narrator tells us that, despite the "gloom" (1.1) of the apartment, he cherished it because it "was a place of [his] own" (1.1) and it was the location where he was going to become a writer.
- As the narrator reminisces about his old place, he remembers Holly Golightly (this is the first time we hear of this very important character). He explains that she lived in the same building in the apartment below his and that the two of them used to go to the bar down the street "six, seven times a day" (1.3). This sounds like they're a bunch of drunks, but it turns out that more often than not they go to the bar to use the phone since they don't have their own.
- Joe Bell ran the bar in those days, and it turns out that he still runs the bar when our story picks up. The narrator tells us quite a bit about Joe. To start, the guy's not married, he's not very easy to get along with, and "he's a hard man to talk to" (1.4). And there are a few things that are "his fixations" (1.4): Holly, hockey, Weimaraners (those are the gray dogs with the blue eyes), a radio soap, and Gilbert and Sullivan (they wrote musicals and operas in the late nineteenth and early twentieth centuries).
- The narrator hasn't talked to Joe in years, so when he gets a call from Joe out of the blue, he figures it has something to do with Holly. Joe asks the narrator to come down to the bar,

which he does, and when he arrives he finds Joe there arranging flowers (apparently this is something Joe has always done).

- Joe tells the narrator that he wouldn't have called him unless it was pretty important, and the narrator assumes that Joe has "heard from Holly" (1.9), which tells us that neither of them has stayed in touch with her. The mention of Holly's name makes Joe's "complexion [which] seems permanently sunburned [… grow] even redder" (1.10). (Sound's like Joe's got a bit of a crush, doesn't it?)

- Joe actually hasn't heard from Holly, but he asks the narrator if he remembers a man named Mr. I.Y. Yunioshi. The narrator remembers him as a photographer who lived in his old apartment building, and it turns out that Yunioshi came into Joe's bar the night before after spending two years in Africa.

- Joe hands the narrator an envelope with three photographs in it (that we can assume Yunioshi took and then left with Joe). The pictures are "more or less the same, though taken from different angles: a tall delicate Negro man wearing a calico skirt and with a shy, yet vain smile, displaying in his hands an odd wood sculpture, an elongated carving of a head, a girl's, her hair sleek and short as a young man's, her smooth wood eyes too large and tilted in the tapering face, her mouth wide overdrawn, not unlike clown-lips" (1.17). It turns out that this carving is the "spit-image of Holly Golightly" (1.17).

- At this point, Joe recounts for the narrator and for us the story behind the statue and the photographs. It seems that Yunioshi was passing through the African village of Tococul when he saw a man "carving monkeys on a walking stick" (1.23). The photographer finds the carvings quite impressive and wants to see more of the man's carvings. The villager shows him the carving of Holly, causing the photographer to feel "as if he were falling in a dream" (1.23). (Holly seems to have quite a hold on Yunioshi, too.) Yunioshi wants to buy the carving, but the villager "cupped his private parts in his hand (apparently a tender gesture, comparable to tapping one's heart) and said no" (1.23). (Let's recount here: so far, Joe Bell, Yunioshi, the villager, and probably the narrator seem to have a thing for Holly, who we still haven't met. This lady sounds pretty intriguing, doesn't she?)

- The villager refuses to sell the carving no matter what Yunioshi offers him, but he does finally agree to tell him how he met the girl in the carving. Apparently, "in the spring of that year a party of three white persons had appeared out of the brush riding horseback" (1.24), a woman and two men who were sick with a fever. The men were shut away in a tent and quarantined while the woman, who we can assume is Holly, "[took] a fancy to the wood-carver, [and] shared the wood-carver's mat" (1.23). We're not exactly sure what this "sharing" means, but Joe seems to think it's something sexual since he feels compelled to tell the narrator that he doesn't believe this part of the story: "'I don't credit that part,' Joe Bell said squeamishly. 'I know she had her ways, but I don't think she'd be up to anything as much as that'" (1.24).

- At some point, Holly just rides away from the village, and the wood-carver doesn't seem to know where she's gone. Yunioshi travels throughout Africa trying to find her, but he never hears another word about her whereabouts. However, Joe seems pretty desperate to have some word about Holly, and he declares Yunioshi's story as the only " *definite* news" (1.28) he's had of her in years. He decides that "She must be rich […] [since] you got to be rich to go mucking around in Africa" (1.28). But perhaps more telling of his character is that he "hope[s] she's rich" (1.28). (Joe seems to be kind of a teddy bear when it comes to Holly, despite the narrator's description of the guy as pretty difficult to get along with).

- The narrator is decidedly less willing to believe that Holly has been having adventures in

Africa, and he sounds pretty bitter when he tells Joe that she's probably "Dead. Or in a crazy house. Or married. I think she's married right in this very city" (1.31). (Pretty interesting that he lumps together being married and being dead or crazy, right?)

- Joe thinks about this for a minute, but he decides that he would have seen Holly if she was still in New York, especially because he's actually been looking for her for more than ten years. He "see[s] pieces of her all the time, a flat little bottom, any skinny girl that walks fast and straight'" (1.32), but he never actually sees Holly.

- Joe's revelation that he's been searching for Holly makes the narrator realize that the bar-keep was in love with her, and while Joe admits to this, he is also careful to make clear that "[...] it wasn't that [he] wanted to touch her" (1.35). He tells the narrator that as he ages, he thinks more and more about sex, but this wasn't the case with Holly: "And I swear it never crossed my mind about Holly. You can love somebody without it being like that. You keep them a stranger, a stranger who's a friend" (1.35). (Joe gets more and more likeable, don't you think?)

- A couple of guys enter the bar, so the narrator gets ready to leave. Joe wants to know if he believes that Holly was ever in Africa, but it doesn't really seem to matter since, "Anyway, she's gone" (1.39). The narrator walks past the old brownstone building and looks at the mailboxes to see who still lives there who he knows (apparently, it's just a woman named Madame Sapphia Spanella), and he remembers that, "It was one of these mailboxes that had first made [him] aware of Holly Golightly" (1.41).

Chapter 2

- We get to meet Holly in this short but rather telling chapter. The narrator first notices her mailbox after living in the apartment for a week, and it's the mailbox name-card that draws his attention. The printed card reads "' *Miss Holiday Golightly*'; and underneath, in the corner, *Traveling*" (2.1). Something about this sticks with the narrator, "like a tune" (2.1).

- The narrator then recalls the night he first actually sees Holly. It's after midnight and Mr. Yunioshi wakes him up when he yells down to Holly, "Miss Golightly! I must protest!" (2.2). It seems that Holly has lost her keys to the front door of the apartment and has rung Yunioshi's bell to get him to let her in. She apparently does this all the time and the photographer angrily reminds her that he needs his sleep since he has a job. She implores him not to be angry and teases him by telling him that she "might let [him] take those pictures [they] mentioned" (2.7). (Pretty racy!) When he asks her when they can take the pictures, she just tells him, "Sometime" (2.10).

- The narrator tries to catch a glimpse of Holly without her seeing him, and he gives us a pretty detailed description of her. She has "ragbag colors [in] her boy's hair, tawny streaks, strands of albino-blond and yellow" (2.21) and she's dressed in "a slim cool black dress, black sandals, a pearl choker" (2.12) (This is the look that Audrey Hepburn made famous in the film version.) She's quite thin, and "[has] an almost breakfast-cereal air of health, a soap and lemon cleanness, a rough pink darkening in the cheeks. Her mouth [is] large, her nose upturned." And "a pair of dark glasses blot[s] out her eyes" (2.12), even though it's the middle of the night. The narrator finds it hard to figure out Holly's age since she looks older than a child but younger than a grown woman (it turns out that she's

almost nineteen at this point).

- Holly has a man with her who is "short and vast" (2.13), and when they get to her apartment the narrator sees this man kiss Holly's neck (she doesn't seem to notice the man, however). Holly thanks him for walking her home and starts to close the door to her apartment. The man protests, and when Holly calls him by the wrong name (his name is Sid Arbuck and she calls him Harry), it's pretty clear that Sid expects something in return for paying for dinner for Holly and her friends: "Didn't I pick up the check, five people, *your* friends, I never seen them before? Don't that give me the right you should like me? You like me, baby" (2.18). Clearly, he's interested in more than just "liking" Holly.
- Holly won't open the door, and Sid gets ready to kick it in (real charmer, isn't he?) but instead falls down the stairs. Holly hears the commotion and opens the door to her apartment, which Sid thinks is a sign that she's changed her mind and wants to "like" him after all. But she quickly put him in his place when she tells him, "Oh, Mr. *Ar*buck. [...] The next time a girl wants a little powder-room change [...] take my advice, darling*don't* give her twenty-cents!" (2.22). We're not exactly sure what to make of this comment, but it seems like Holly is accusing Sid of being cheap.

Chapter 3

- Instead of bugging Yunioshi when she forgets her keys, Holly starts bugging the narrator by ringing *his* apartment at all hours of the night. At first, the narrator thinks that every time the bell rings it's "bad news, a telegram" (3.1), but he soon gets used to Holly saying, "'Sorry darling – I forgot my key'" (3.1). Don't you just love how she calls him "darling" when she's only nineteen?
- Even though Holly has no problem bugging the narrator, the two haven't actually talked to each other in person at this point. The narrator sees Holly all the time when he's out walking around the neighborhood, but she doesn't recognize him as the man who lets her into the apartment building at three o'clock in the morning. In fact, "she seem[s] not quite to see [him] at all" when they meet on the street (3.2). Holly, it seems, is wrapped up in her own little world.
- We learn a little more about what Holly looks like from the narrator (maybe it's because he's a writer that he notices all these small details about her, or perhaps he finds her attractive). Holly always wears dark glasses, she always looks well put-together, "there [is] a consequential good taste in the plainness of her clothes, the blues and grays that made her, herself, shine so" (3.2). There's something special about Holly that comes not from her clothes or from her dark glasses, but from within the person.
- The narrator also remembers seeing Holly at the famous restaurant "21" one night. She's with a bunch of men who remind the narrator of our good friend Mr. Arbuck (remember the guy who fell down the stairs?), and Holly looks utterly bored. He also sees her at a saloon being passed from soldier to soldier as they dance and sing. Clearly, men like Holly very much and pay a lot of attention to her when she's out and about.
- The narrator still doesn't meet Holly throughout the summer, but he gets to know her a little better by paying attention to the things she throws away in her wastebasket (this sounds creepier than it really is. Holly's just the kind of girl that people want to know more

about. She's kind of illusive and mysterious, and even though the narrator seems like a little bit of a stalker, we think he's really just intrigued by her). He finds "tabloids and travel folders and astrological charts" (3.4), the wrappers from her cigarettes, leftover "cottage cheese and melba toast" (3.4) and hair dye. He also finds loads of "V-letters," which are letters from soldiers overseas (don't forget, World War II is taking place during the story), and many of them profess their love for Holly.

- Holly also has a cat, and sometimes when she's letting her hair dry she'll sit on the fire escape with him and play the guitar and sing. She often sings "the show hits" and really likes the songs from *Oklahoma!*, but she also sings songs that seem to have a little more meaning, "songs that made you wonder where she learned them, where indeed she came from. Harsh-tender wandering tunes with words that smacked of pineywoods or prairie" (3.5). Holly Golightly, it appears, wasn't always a city girl, and although she seems pretty flaky and flighty at times, there is clearly more to her than meets the eye.

- Finally, the narrator and Holly come face-to-face one night in September. The narrator has crawled into bed with a drink and a book when he suddenly gets the feeling that someone's watching him. He hears "an abrupt rapping at the window" (3.6) and then spills his drink when he sees a shadow outside. It turns out to be Holly.

- When the narrator opens the window, Holly climbs into his room and tells him that she has a horrible man down in her apartment. Apparently he gets pretty mean when he's drinking (Holly shows the narrator a bite mark on her shoulder from her drunk visitor), and Holly climbs out of the bathroom window – not because she's scared of him, but because she's tired of dealing with him. When she sees the narrator looking all "cozy" (3.7) in bed, she can't resist knocking on his window since it's so cold outside.

- It seems the narrator reminds Holly of her brother Fred, and that's the other reason she knocks on his window. Holly and her siblings "used to sleep four in a bed, and [Fred] was the only one that ever let [her] hug him on a cold night" (3.7). She asks the narrator if she can call him Fred, which he never really answers, but she starts calling him Fred anyway (so now our narrator has a name, sort of).

- As Holly tells the new Fred about her brother Fred, she makes her way farther and farther into the bedroom and declares, "I suppose you think I'm very brazen" (3.7). When the narrator replies, "Not at all" (3.8), Holly "seem[s] disappointed" (3.9). It seems she likes the disapproval she often experiences from others.

- Holly comments on the décor in the narrator's apartment by calling it a "chamber of horrors" (3.10), and asks how he can stand living there (she doesn't hold much back, does she?). When the narrator says that a person can "get used to anything" (3.11), Holly's reply to this tells us a lot about her. She declares that a person who allows himself or herself to get used to things "might as well be dead" (3.12), which hints at Holly's chaotic lifestyle. She seems to like change, to like new things and people around her all the time, and to never be in one place long enough to get used to it.

- As Holly and the narrator continue talking, she reveals that she "can't get excited by a man until he's forty-two" (3.16). Someone she knows thinks this means that Holly has a "father complex" (3.16), but Holly says that she's "simply *trained* [herself] to like older men" (3.16).

- Talk turns back to her brother Fred, and Holly tells the narrator that she hasn't seen her brother since she left home at fourteen. When he asks her why she left at such a young age, Holly looks at him without answering and rubs her nose. Eventually, the narrator learns that this is Holly's way of saying that "one was trespassing" (3.23) – that a person is

getting a little too close for comfort: "Like many people with a bold fondness for volunteering intimate information, anything that suggested a direct question, a pinning-down, put her on guard" (3.23). Holly will share information about herself, but only what she wants to share and only on her terms. When she gets uncomfortable with the narrator's question, she quickly changes the subject and asks him to tell her about one of the stories he's written.

- He reads her his most recent story about two women who live together as roommates. One of the women gets engaged, and in order to stop the wedding, the other woman spreads rumors about the first. When the narrator finishes reading, Holly doesn't have the reaction he hopes for. She thinks the story is about lesbians: "'Of course I like dykes themselves. They don't scare me a bit. But stories about dykes bore the bejesus out of me. I just can't put myself in their shoes" (3.29). When the narrator looks confused, Holly asks, "Well really, darling… if it's not about a couple of old bull-dykes, what the hell *is* it about?" (3.29). Holly isn't very PC here, and she clearly misunderstands what the narrator intended his story to be about, but we kind of have to appreciate her bluntness. She certainly doesn't sugar-coat anything, does she?

- Holly, still completely unaware that she's misunderstood his story, asks the narrator if he "happen[s] to *know* any nice lesbians" (3.31) since she's "looking for a roommate" (3.31). She tells him (again blissfully unconcerned with being PC) that "dykes are wonderful home-makers, they love to do all the work, you never have to bother about brooms and defrosting and sending out the laundry" (3.31). She tells him that she used to live with a lesbian and that people then thought she was gay, too. But she isn't bothered by this, and even tells the narrator that perhaps she is gay: "And of course I am. Everyone is: a bit. So what?" (3.31). So, despite using language that probably makes most of us cringe, Holly seems pretty accepting and open about sexuality.

- As the sun comes up, Holly realizes that she's late for a standing appointment at Sing Sing prison (she just gets more and more interesting, doesn't she?). It seems that she gets paid to visit Sally Tomato, a man who's in jail for alleged mafia activities. She tells the narrator, though, that she "adores" (3.43) Sally so much that she would probably go visit him without the money.

- We then get the story of how Holly came to be the paid visitor of Sally Tomato. Remember Joe Bell's bar from the first chapter? Well, Sally used to hang out in the back of Joe's bar and he apparently took a liking to Holly. When he's later sent to prison, he has his "lawyer" (Holly's pretty sure he isn't a lawyer at all since they always meet at a hamburger joint) contact Holly and the man offers to pay her one hundred dollars a week to "cheer up a lonely old man" (3.45). Holly assumes that she's being asked to do something unseemly and quickly rejects the offer since she isn't "a nurse that does tricks on the side" (3.45). Plus, she knows she can earn more just by asking her dates for money for the ladies room (who knew going to the ladies room could be such a lucrative business?). But the lawyer tells Holly that Sally has admired her for a long time, so Holly agrees because "it [is] too romantic" (3.45).

- This all seems innocent enough, but as we get a little more of the story it seems that Holly's visits serve another purpose besides just keeping old Sally company. The only way she gets paid is to leave messages about the weather for the "lawyer" (we learn here that his name is Mr. O'Shaughnessy). Holly assumes that these messages are just ways for O'Shaughnessy to make sure she's actually been to the prison, but it becomes pretty clear that Sally is passing information to his "lawyer" through Holly. The narrator expresses

concern about the arrangement, but Holly blows him off and tells him that she can take care of herself.

- Holly eventually makes her way to the bed and asks the narrator if she can lie down next him, just "to rest a moment" (3.55). She tells him to go to sleep, which he pretends to do, and eventually he feels Holly touch his arm very carefully, thinking it won't wake him up. When she starts to whisper something, he first thinks she's talking to him, but it quickly becomes clear that she's pining for her brother Fred: "Poor Fred. [. . .] Where are you, Fred? Because it's cold. There's snow in the wind" (3.56).

- At this point, Holly lays her head on the narrator's shoulder and starts to cry (she isn't as carefree as she seems, is she?). When he asks her why she's crying she replies, "I *hate* snoops" (3.58), and she quickly gets up and heads for the fire escape (it seems he's caught her in a moment of vulnerability and this makes her very, very uncomfortable).

Chapter 4

- This is an interesting chapter because not a lot happens in the way of action but we learn a ton more personal information about Holly.

- After the night in the narrator's bedroom, Holly stops ringing his apartment when she loses her key, and he realizes that he misses her. He starts to feel lonely, but he doesn't want to see his old friends since they seem plain and boring now; he calls them a "salt-free, sugarless diet" (4.1). The narrator gets so distracted by thoughts of Holly that he's no longer able to write, so he eventually sends her a message to remind her to visit Sally in prison the next day. Holly thanks him by inviting him to her apartment for a drink.

- When the narrator arrives, he's greeted by a man who he describes in detail as a "creature" (4.3). "His bald freckled head was dwarf-big: attached to it were a pair of pointed, truly elfin ears. He had Pekingese eyes, unpitying and slightly bulged. Tufts of hair sprouted from his ears, from his nose; his jowls were gray with afternoon beard, and his handshake almost furry" (4.3). The guy sounds like a mix between an elf and a dog, doesn't he?

- This is the first time the narrator has seen the inside of Holly's apartment, and it looks like she's just moved in. Nothing is unpacked, there really isn't any furniture, and it has the "fly-by-night look" (4.4) we might expect of Holly.

- Holly's still in the shower, so the narrator and the elf-dog start chatting, and this is when we learn a lot about Holly's past. Apparently, Holly believes in a lot of what the elf-dog thinks is "crap" (4.16) (though we never get a clear explanation of what that stuff is). At one time a man named Benny Polan, who is "respected everywhere" (4.16), wanted to marry her, and he sent her to countless "head-shrinkers" (4.16) to rid her of her "ideas" (4.16). It seems even Freud couldn't cure Holly. The elf-dog finds all of this incredibly frustrating and he finally declares that one day Holly is going to wind up addicted to pills.

- As the conversation continues, we hear of additional "opportunities" that Holly has passed up. We find out that the elf-dog is actually an important Hollywood agent named O.J. Berman. Apparently, at some point he had secured a role in a big movie for Holly after discovering her at the race track.

- When Berman first sees Holly, she has been going to the horse races every day because

she's living with one of the jockeys. Holly is fifteen years old at the time, so Berman threatens to turn the jockey in to the police unless he breaks things off with her, which the guy then does. Berman takes Holly under his wing and starts to groom her for work as an actress, and eventually gets her an audition for a Cecil B. DeMille film (he was a very famous director at the time).

- The day before the audition, Berman gets a call from Holly and it seems she has left for New York. He demands that she "get [her] ass on a plane and get back [to Los Angeles]" (4.20), but Holly refuses to return. She tells Berman that she just doesn't want to be famous, and that she doesn't want to be a movie star. When he asks her what she does want, she tells him she doesn't know but that he'll "be the first to know" (4.20) when she figures it out. And that puts an end to Holly's Hollywood career.

- We then hear about Rusty Trawler for the first time (another man who wants to marry Holly), but before we get the whole story Holly comes into the living room wearing just a towel and still dripping wet from the shower. She tells Berman that Fred (the narrator) is a "genius" (4.36) writer and that the agent should help "make [him] rich" (4.36). Nothing really comes of this conversation, though, since the rest of the guests (all men at this point) start to show up.

- Several military officers and older men arrive in the next few minutes, and each one is clearly upset that he's not the only one there (they all seem to want Holly to themselves). But the men start hanging out and enjoying each other's company, and this is when the narrator notices one man in particular – Rusty Trawler.

- The narrator describes Rusty as a man in a child's body. He looks like he's never aged and something about his face reminds the narrator of a little kid on the verge of a temper tantrum. But Rusty is actually a happy host and he spends the evening serving drinks, choosing the music, and introducing the guests to each other. He doesn't even seem to mind when Holly flirts with other men, even though he's supposedly in love with her (but more about this later).

- We then get to hear Rusty's story, and it is a doozy. Both of his parents died when he was five, and they left him millions of dollars. He also became a bit of a tabloid celebrity. As a young boy, Rusty "had caused his godfather-custodian to be arrested on charges of sodomy" (4.41), and his series of marriages and divorces became the stuff of tabloid stories. He has been married and divorced four times so far, and it was rumored that he asked Unity Mitford to marry him too (she was a real-life friend of Hitler's and supported the fascist movement). It seems Rusty has some fascist tendencies himself since he also attends what we can assume are fascist rallies. And this is what we learn of the man who now wants to marry Holly.

- Holly eventually takes some time out of flirting with her guests to come talk to the narrator, and she really encourages him to pursue things with Berman since he can help the narrator's career as a writer (it seems that Holly has developed true affection for the man who reminds her of her brother).

- He asks her about the part in the DeMille movie, and Holly tells him that she "knew damn well [she'd] never be a movie star" (4.51). It's more important to her to be herself and to "have [her] ego tagging along" (4.51) when she does become rich and famous, which she fully intends to do at some point in her life (got to love her self-confidence!) And it's in this conversation that we first hear of Tiffany's when Holly declares, "I want to still be me when I wake up one fine morning and have breakfast at Tiffany's" (4.51).

- The conversation shifts very briefly to Holly's cat, who she refuses to name since she

doesn't "have any right to give him one" (4.52). Holly doesn't consider the cat as *belonging* to her and says she doesn't "want to own anything until [she] know[s] [she's] found the place where [she] and things belong together" (4.52). Although this seems like an insignificant detail, this cat without a name, it tells us a lot about Holly and her aversion to being tied down by anything or anyone.

- Talk shifts back to Tiffany's, and we learn why Holly likes the upscale jewelry store so much. It's not the expensive things in it but rather that the store makes Holly feel better when she's got what she calls the "mean reds" (4.55). When she's feeling afraid and is sure that "something bad is going to happen" (5.54), she goes to Tiffany's and the place makes her feel better.

- She mentions her brother Fred again, and it's pretty clear that she imagines this real-life place as one for her and her brother. All Holly wants, it seems, is a place to feel safe, and she hasn't found that spot yet.

- At this point, Rusty comes up and interrupts the conversation. He acts like a child with Holly and teases her about not loving him. She responds to him as if she were his "governess" (4.62), reminding him of his "chores" (4.66) and chiding him about his diet. He seems satisfied by this and returns to the party, and then Holly tells the narrator that Rusty is gay. He won't admit it, but perhaps this is why he doesn't seem too bothered that she flirts with other men in front of him.

- An interesting shift in action occurs at this point when Mag Wildwood enters (she's a model who poses for Yunioshi), and it's clear that Holly doesn't like this woman one bit. Mag pushes her way through the crowd of men and latches on to Berman, but all of the other men want her attention as well. She's not particularly beautiful, but she's really tall and seems to have embraced her "defects" (4.89) by drawing attention to them, which intrigues people. She wears high heels even though she towers over everyone else, she dresses in tight-fitting clothes that accentuate her boyish figure, and she wears her hair in such a way that "accentuat[es] the spareness, the starvation of her fashion-model face" (4.89). She also stutters, but even this behavior seems exaggerated. The effect of all of this is that the men in Holly's apartment are immediately drawn to Mag, which just seems to bug Holly to no end.

- When Mag excuses herself and goes to the restroom, Holly takes this opportunity to crush the model when she tells her guests the following: "'It's really very sad.' She paused long enough to calculate the number of inquiring expressions; it was sufficient. 'And so mysterious. You'd think it would show more. But heaven knows she *looks* healthy. So, well, *clean*. That's the extraordinary part. Wouldn't you [...] wouldn't you say she *looked* clean?'" (4.90). Holly never specifies what exactly she's referring to here, but we can guess that she's implying that Mag has a sexually-transmitted disease (hence the suggestion that she's unclean).

- This revelation has the desired effect and when Mag returns to the party there is a noticeable shift. The men are cold and no longer interested in her, and "more unforgivably, people were leaving without taking her telephone number" (4.93). Since she's already drunk, Mag reacts belligerently. She calls Holly a "Hollywood degenerate" (4.93), then tells Berman (who we can assume is Jewish) that "Hitler was right" (4.93), and she physically threatens Rusty. She eventually falls to the floor and won't get up, so Holly asks the narrator to get Mag a taxi and send her home. Holly and the rest of the men leave, and Mag tries to get up, but she passes out and the narrator leaves her there to sleep it off.

Chapter 5

- Even though Holly didn't seem to like Mag much the night before, when she runs into the narrator the next day she lets him know that Mag is still in her apartment and Holly seems pretty sympathetic that her guest has "a hang-over out to here" (5.1).
- Soon after, we're introduced to Mag's fiancée, who the narrator describes as "the Latin who came to [his] door, mistakenly" (5.1). He is a handsome man with a "bullfighter's figure" and a "bashful manner" (5.1), and he arrives one day with a lot of suitcases, which intrigues the narrator.
- On the following Sunday, the narrator hears Holly and Mag on the fire escape and the two women are chatting while waiting for their hair to dry (it seems Holly has changed her mind about Mag a little). Talk quickly turns to the men in their lives.
- Mag thinks that Holly is lucky to have Rusty since, at the very least, "he's an American" (5.4). Holly doesn't seem very impressed by this, but Mag tells her that this is indeed a big deal since they're in the middle of a war. Mag considers herself quite the patriot and stutters to Holly that she's "p-p-proud of [her] country" (5.8) (not surprisingly, Holly doesn't seem to share this sentiment).
- Holly briefly mentions her brother Fred, who's a soldier in the war, but Mag thinks she's referring to the narrator. Mag tells Holly that she thinks the narrator "look[s] stupid" (5.10). Holly corrects her, though, and says that the narrator simply has the look of "yearning" (5.11) since he's on the outside looking in and "He wants awfully to be on the inside staring out" (5.11).
- Mag then starts talking about her fiancée, José, who is Brazilian, and it seems that Mag will be moving to his home country with him since he wants to be Brazil's president. She declares that she "'must be madly in love'" (5.18), and while this all sounds very romantic, Holly is more interested in learning about their sex life and the conversation turns a little bawdy.
- Holly wants to know if José bites Mag during sex, which he apparently does not, but Mag tells her that he does laugh during sex, which Holly appreciates. As Holly presses for more details, Mag tells her that she really can't remember, so Holly suggests that she "try leaving the lights on" (5.29) so that she has something to look at. Mag's a little embarrassed about this and tells Holly that she's actually a "very-very-very *conventional* person" (5.30), but Holly reveals that she sees nothing wrong with looking at men when they're naked since "men are beautiful" (5.31).
- Mag eventually reaches the conclusion that she really does love José, but she laments the "Heat. Rain. J-jungles" (5.38) that await her in Brazil. Holly says that she'd enjoy that, and Mag replies, "Better you than me" (5.40), which Holly agrees with.

Chapter 6

- The narrator gets a letter from "a small university review to whom [he'd] sent a story" (6.1), and they want to publish it, even though they can't pay him for the piece. He's so excited

he's "dizzy" (6.1), and races to Holly's apartment to share the good news. It seems pretty clear that he's come to value his friendship with Holly a great deal since she's now the first person he thinks to tell about being a published writer.

- When she answers the door, the narrator is too excited to talk so he just hands her the letter. After taking way too long to read it, Holly doesn't give the narrator the reaction he had hoped for. She tells him that he shouldn't let them publish his story without giving him some money for it (after all, this is the girl who demands money for going to the ladies room when she's out on a date. Of course she wouldn't publish something for free). In a surprisingly perceptive moment, Holly realizes that she has disappointed the narrator, and she quickly invites him to lunch to celebrate.

- While the narrator waits for Holly to get dressed, he gets a chance to see her bedroom (nothing seedy here – she just leaves the bedroom door open while she's getting ready in the bathroom). Her bedroom looks just like her living room, with "everything packed and ready to go, like the belongings of a criminal who feels the law not far behind" (6.3). The one big difference is that the bedroom has actual furniture in it – a bed. It's "a double one at that, and quite flashy: blond wood, tufted satin" (6.3). (What should we make of her fancy bed as the one piece of real furniture in the apartment? We're not exactly sure, but it seems like an important detail.)

- As Holly brushes her teeth, she tells the narrator that Mag is her new roommate and, even though she isn't a lesbian (which Holly would prefer), Mag is "the next best thing" (6.4) because she's "a *perfect* fool" (6.4). This means Holly can make her do all the chores and leave her with the lease if she decides to bolt all of a sudden (so maybe she hasn't really changed her mind about Mag but just sees her as easy to take advantage of).

- As this conversation continues, Holly digs around her messy room for her shoes, her shirt, and her belt. The narrator wonders how Holly is able to always look so polished and put-together despite the "wreckage" (6.6) of her room, and he describes her as always looking "pampered, calmly immaculate, as though she's been attended by Cleopatra's maids" (6.6).

- This chapter ends with a final, really sweet moment between Holly and the narrator. She "cup[s] her hand under [his] chin" and tells him, "I'm glad about the story. Really I am" (6.6).

Chapter 7

- This chapter is set in October 1943, and it's "a beautiful day with the buoyancy of a bird" (7.1). Holly and the narrator spend the day together in the city – they have drinks at Joe Bell's bar, watch a parade on Fifth Avenue, eat lunch in the park, and walk around the lake. They don't go to the zoo (it sounds as though they're in Central Park) because Holly can't "bear to see anything in a cage" (7.1), but they spend the afternoon talking about each other's childhoods.

- Surprisingly, Holly talks about her childhood, but not so surprisingly, she reveals nothing specific. The narrator describes it as "elusive, nameless, placeless, an impressionistic recital" (7.2). The picture she paints isn't what the narrator expects from a girl who ran away from home at fourteen – it's "an almost voluptuous account of swimming and

summer, Christmas trees, pretty cousins and parties: in short, happy in a way that she was not" (7.2). We never know if Holly is making this up or if she's describing her actual childhood, but the narrator doesn't think it goes with the girl he knows.

- Talking about her childhood reminds Holly of her brother Fred, and she decides that she wants to send him some peanut butter since it's such a rare treat during the war (take a look at Shmoop's US History guide to " World War II: Home Front" to find out about what things were like in the U.S. during the war).

- They're able to scrape together just a few jars of peanut butter (guess we shouldn't take those jars of Skippy for granted, should we?) and then the narrator takes Holly to an antique store to see the elaborate bird cage that he admired when he first moved to the apartment. Holly appreciates the "fantasy" (7.4) of it, but she doesn't really like it since "[...] still, it's a cage" (7.4) (she really, really doesn't like feeling closed in, does she?).

- They keep walking around the city and Holly decides that they should do a little shoplifting for fun. Since it's October there are Halloween decorations in the local Woolworth's, so they go in, they each put a mask on, and then they simply walk out of the drugstore.

- Once they're out of the store, they run "to make it more dramatic" (7.5), and the narrator realizes that he likes the feeling of stealing something, that "successful theft exhilarates" (7.5). The narrator asks Holly if she's done much shoplifting and she tells him that she used to have to steal but now she just does it "sort of to keep [her] hand in" (7.5).

- In a final detail that seems pretty important, the narrator tells us that he and Holly "wore masks all the way home" (7.6).

Chapter 8

- The narrator has to get a nine-to-five job (it's not easy being a writer), so he doesn't get to see much of Holly since their hours are now so different (she's usually still asleep or just waking up when he gets home). His neighbor's always headed out the door for a night out, most often with Rusty, Mag, and José.

- The narrator doesn't think that José fits with the rest of the group (we learn that his full name is José Ybarra-Jaegar, by the way) since "he was intelligent, he was presentable, he appeared to have a serious link with his work, which was obscurely governmental, vaguely important, and took him to Washington several days a week" (8.2), but he seems to enjoy their company nonetheless. The narrator comes to the conclusion that, because he's not American, José doesn't really make distinctions between the Americans he meets, so his friends seem "to be tolerable examples of local color and national character" (8.2). He also realizes that "Holly's determination" (8.2) keeps José around, too (we'll hear more about this later).

- One day, the narrator sees Holly going into the public library, which strikes him as odd since "Holly and libraries were not an easy association to make" (8.3). He follows her into the building (again, seeming kind of creepy but he's just more curious than anything), and this prompts some interesting meditations on his part about people's personalities.

- As he watches Holly flip through mountains of books, he starts to think about a girl he once knew named Mildred Grossman. Mildred and Holly couldn't be more different since Mildred is a "top-heavy realist" (8.3) and Holly is a "lopsided romantic" (8.3). But, for some

reason, the two "acquired a Siamese twinship" (8.3) in the narrator's mind since, unlike the "average personality that reshapes frequently" (8.3), Holly and Mildred will never change. He determines that Holly will always be exactly as she is now.

- The narrator gets sort of lost in his thoughts until he sees Holly get up to leave. He heads to the table where she was sitting and finds a ton of books about Brazil (she's obviously trying to learn about José's world, but we don't really know why yet. Maybe Mag should be worried!).

- The chapter shifts to Christmas Eve and Holly and Mag invite the narrator to their apartment for a party. The group decorates a huge Christmas tree with ornaments and tinsel and some balloons that Holly steals from Woolworth's (nothing like tradition around the holidays, right?), and Holly tells the narrator that she has a gift for him.

- The gift turns out to be the antique bird cage the narrator showed Holly on their day out in the city, and he's horrified that she would spend so much money on him (it costs $350). But Holly brushes this off as just "a few extra trips to the powder room" (8.8). She makes the narrator promise that he'll "never put a living thing in it" (8.8), but she's glad she can give him the gift.

- The narrator leans in to kiss Holly (we can't tell if this is a friendly peck or something more), but she stops him by demanding the gift he has for her. The narrator gives her a St. Christopher's medal from Tiffany's, which he assumes in later years that she loses since "Holly was not a girl who could keep anything" (8.10). On the flip side, we learn that he keeps the birdcage with him for years as he travels around the country and the world.

- Things take sort of nasty turn here as the narrator describes the "big falling-out" he has with Holly (8.10) after she gets back from a winter vacation with Mag, Rusty, and José.

- We first get to hear about the trip from Holly. The four travelers start in Key West where Rusty gets into a fight with some sailors and has to "wear a spine brace the rest of his life" (8.11). Mag also has a horrible trip since she gets first-degree burns from being out in the sun and subsequently has to stay in the hospital, covered in "blisters and citronella" (8.11). Ever the caring friends (we're being sarcastic here), Holly and José leave Mag and Rusty in Key West and head to Havana, Cuba, a city that Holly loves.

- Once they get back to Florida, Mag is convinced that Holly and José have been having an affair until Holly convinces Mag that she's gay (we don't know if anything happens between Holly and José in Cuba, but it's possible, right?).

- Holly tells the narrator all of this while they're in her apartment. It's March and the Christmas tree is still in the living room. Holly wants to "preserve her tropic look" (8.12) from the trip, so she asks the narrator to rub oil on her back while she lies under a sun lamp, which he does.

- She tells him that she passed one of his stories to O.J. Berman, who "was quite impressed" (8.16). But Berman doesn't think the narrator should continue to write about "Negroes and children" (8.16) since no one cares about these things. Holly apparently agrees with Berman and refers to the characters in the narrator's story as "brats and niggers" (8.18). She doesn't think his stories " *mean* anything" (8.18).

- This is when the falling out happens. As the narrator rubs oil on Holly's back and has to listen to her criticize his writing, he has the overwhelming urge to spank her like child – "My hand, smoothing oil on her skin, seemed to have a temper of its own: it yearned to raise itself and come down on her buttocks" (8.19). This sounds potentially sexual, and it might be, but the narrator is clearly angry at this point.

- He asks Holly for an example of a story "that means something" (8.19), and she replies

with *Wuthering Heights*. This makes him want to hit her even more since she's comparing his writing to "a work of genius" (8.21), but when it becomes clear that she's only seen the movie and never read the book the narrator feels better. He seems relieved (as he describes it), and Holly takes this as a sense of superiority on his part. "Her muscles hardened, the touch of her was like stone warmed by the sun. 'Everybody has to feel superior to somebody,' she said. 'But it's customary to present a little proof before you take the privilege'" (8.24).

- The narrator tells Holly that he doesn't compare himself to her or to Berman, "therefore, [he] can't feel superior" (8.25). He says he doesn't want the same things they want (like money), and Holly realizes that this is a criticism of her. She warns him that it would be in his best interest to want money since he has "an expensive imagination" (8.28) and since "not many people are going to buy [him] bird cages" (8.28).
- He offers a half-hearted apology, and Holly tells him that he really will be sorry if he hits her. She elaborates, "You wanted to a minute ago: I could feel it in your hand; and you want to now" (8.30). And the narrator does want to hit her at that moment. He tells her that he wouldn't be sorry if he hit her but that he is sorry she spent so much money on his Christmas gift since "Rusty Trawler is too hard a way of earning it" (8.31). Although we get no intimation that Holly sleeps with Rusty for money (especially because she's convinced he's gay), the narrator all but accuses her of acting like a prostitute, and this is the last straw for Holly. She gives him two seconds to get out of her apartment, and he leaves with both of them angry with each other.

Chapter 9

- After their argument, the narrator decides "to put Holly Golightly absolutely out of [his] life" (9.1). He heads up to his apartment, grabs the bird cage, and leaves it in front of Holly's apartment. He thinks he's teaching her a lesson, but when he sees the cage in the trash the next day, he secretly takes it back up to his place (guess he showed her!).
- Things are pretty awkward and tense between the two after this. When they see each other in the apartment building they avoid eye contact, and if the narrator ever sees Holly at Joe Bell's, he leaves the bar. Things continue on in this manner until the narrator notices a strange man outside of her apartment one day.
- Although the narrator's used to seeing all sorts of men at Holly's apartment, he spots a "*very* provocative man examining her mailbox" (9.3). The man is "a person in his early fifties with a hard, weathered face, gray forlorn eyes. He wore an old sweat-stained gray hat, and his cheap summer suit, a pale blue, hung too loosely on his lanky frame; his shoes were brown and brand-new" (9.3). He doesn't ring Holly's doorbell, but keeps touching "the embossed lettering of her name" (9.3) on the door.
- The narrator notices this man again later in the evening and he starts to wonder who he is. Maybe he's a detective or "some underworld agent connected with her Sing Sing friend, Sally Tomato" (9.4). Although he's still angry with her, the thought of Holly being watched by some seedy guy makes the narrator worry and he decides to tell her that someone is watching her.
- As the narrator heads to dinner, he realizes that the man is following him and whistling the

same song that Holly plays on her guitar and sings to. When the narrator enters the restaurant, the man follows him and sits down right next to him. The narrator decides to confront him and ask him what it is that he wants, and the man replies, "Son, [...] I need a friend" (9.7).

- The man shows the narrator an old picture of his family. There are six children and the man himself in the picture, and the narrator notices a "plump blond little girl with a hand shading her eyes against the sun" (9.6). The man points himself out to the narrator, points out Fred, and then points out a person who the narrator eventually recognizes as a young Holly. The narrator assumes that this man is Holly's father, but boy is he wrong.

- It turns out that Holly's real name is Lulamae Barnes and that this man is not her father, but her husband. He's a veterinarian from Texas named Doc Golightly and he tells the narrator that he's been searching for Holly ever since she left five years ago. Apparently, Fred sent Holly's New York address to Doc, and this is how the man knows where to find her.

- Doc wants to take Holly home so she can be with "her husband and her churren" (9.13), and it turns out that the four remaining kids in the picture are Holly's stepkids. They're older than she is, but since she married their dad, he believes she should be home acting like a mom.

- It seems Doc married Holly when she was just fourteen, and we get to hear the story of how she and Fred came to live with Doc in the first place. Both of Holly and Fred's parents died from tuberculosis, and Doc's oldest daughter finds them trying to steal milk and eggs one day. The two kids were in terrible health – malnourished, thin, and with rotted teeth. Upon their parents' deaths, the Barnes kids are sent to live with different people, and Holly and Fred end up "with some mean, no-count people" (9.18). This is who they've run away from when they end up at Doc's.

- Life seems to be going OK for Holly and Fred once Doc takes them in. Doc teaches Holly to play the guitar, he teaches a crow to say Holly's name, and he lets Holly lounge around and do whatever she wants while the rest of the kids do all the work. Before he knows it, he falls in love with Holly (mind you, she's still just fourteen), and asks her to marry him, to which she agrees.

- Doc indulges Holly's every wish, including subscribing to every magazine she wants (which he blames for her desire to leave him since she gets to see and read about far-off places). But, soon, Holly starts to wander. She takes long walks every day, but she always comes home. Then the walks get longer and longer until she just doesn't come back one day.

- Fred, however, doesn't leave, and he lives with Doc until he's drafted into the army. It's Fred who stays in touch with Holly and it's Fred who tells Doc where she is in New York. Doc races to New York because he knows Holly "wants to go home" (9.20), but he doesn't want to freak out Holly by confronting her, so he asks the narrator if he'll let Holly know that he's in town.

- Still angry with Holly, the narrator relishes the idea of revealing Doc in front of Holly's friends, but he changes his mind when he sees how hopeful and serious Doc is about a reunion with his wife.

- The narrator does go to Holly's apartment while Doc waits downstairs, and when she answers she assumes the narrator is there to bury the hatchet: "'Well, idiot,' she said, and playfully slapped me with her purse. 'I'm in too much of a hurry to make up now. We'll smoke the pipe tomorrow, okay?'" (9.22).

- The narrator responds by calling her Lulamae, and upon hearing this Holly thinks that Fred has come to New York. She runs into the hall and calls for her brother, but it's Doc who appears. Holly seems more disappointed than anything, and Doc seems "hangdog and shy" (9.25), awkward in front of Holly.
- At first, Holly doesn't seem to recognize Doc, but then she "touch[es] his face; her fingers test […] the reality of his chin, his beard stubble," and she "kisse[s] him on the cheek" (9.26). Doc is so happy to see her that he lifts her up when he hugs her, and the two seem lost in their own little world.

Chapter 10

- We find Holly and the narrator in Joe's bar the next day. Holly is already drunk and it's not even noon, and she and the narrator are talking about Doc.
- Holly tells the narrator that she never considered divorcing Doc since she assumed she was too young for the marriage to be considered legal in the first place, and she also reveals that she and Doc had sex the night before. The narrator is shocked to hear this and, "for the first time since [he'd] known her, [Holly] seemed to feel a need to justify herself" (10.3). She tells the narrator that she and Doc really do love each other after all and he's surprised to learn that Holly has been praying for Doc all these years.
- After sleeping together, Doc and Holly spend the rest of the night in the bus station, and Doc assumes that Holly is going to return to Texas with him. She tries to make him see that she's not the same person as before, but she realizes that, in some ways, she is: "I'm still stealing turkey eggs and running through a brier patch. Only now I call it having the mean reds" (10.5).
- She tells Joe and the narrator that Doc's "mistake" was that he fell in love with a "wild thing" (10.7), and that wild things can't ever be tamed. After getting Doc to finally see this, they part ways amicably (at least according to Holly), and he heads back to Texas without her.
- Holly toasts Doc and says to herself more than to anyone else that the city is "such an empty place; so vague" (10.11), and she's glad that Doc doesn't have to live there.

Chapter 11

- The narrator is on the subway when he sees a newspaper headline announcing that Rusty Trawler has married for the fourth time. He assumes that the lucky girl is Holly, and the thought of this makes him wish he was "under the wheels of the train" (11.1). He's also depressed because he lost his job (he won't tell us why) and can't find a new one, he hasn't seen Holly in weeks, and the draft board has been contacting him. And he finally admits that he is also in love with Holly, "a little" (11.1).
- When he buys his own newspaper and gets to read the rest of the headline, he sees that Rusty has married Mag, not Holly. He's incredibly relieved about this and heads home, but when he gets there he's met with a disturbing scene.

- Madame Spanella, one of the tenants in the building, runs into the narrator and screams at him to get the police since Holly "is killing somebody! [Or] somebody is killing her!" (11.3). He runs to Holly's apartment and bangs on the door. This stops the ruckus inside her apartment, but she still won't open the door.
- Shortly after, José arrives with a doctor and lets himself into the apartment with his key. The place is destroyed. The Christmas tree has been torn apart, broken lamps and records litter the floor, the food from the refrigerator has been thrown everywhere, and Holly has broken all of her perfume bottles. Holly's dark glasses are also broken on the floor, "the lenses already shattered, the frames cracked in half" (11.8).
- Holly's now lying on her bed, and she doesn't seem to recognize José or to even notice the doctor. The doctor asks Holly if she wants to go to sleep, and when she touches her head, she "leav[es] a smear of blood from a cut finger" (11.10). She starts talking about something that the rest of them don't understand: "He's the only one would ever let me. Let me hug him on cold nights. I saw a place in Mexico. With horses. By the sea" (11.10).
- The doctor thinks this is just incoherent mumbling and he injects Holly with a sedative to calm her down. In the meantime, José is trying to understand what's wrong with Holly, and he finally realizes that she's acting like this because of grief. The doctor asks for everyone to leave the room, and José asks the narrator to go have a drink with him.
- He tells the narrator that he's worried "that this [episode with Holly] should cause scandal" (11.19) and that it could damage his political career. He then tells the narrator what actually happened, that Holly was drinking and started throwing the things in her apartment "when the sadness came" (11.21). The narrator thinks that Holly's upset about Rusty and Mag's marriage, but José reveals that he and Holly, who are in a relationship, are thrilled when their significant others take off together. It's clearly not Rusty and Mag's nuptials that makes Holly so upset.
- We then learn what has really caused Holly to react in such a way. José hands the narrator a crumpled telegram that reads: "*Received notice young Fred killed in action overseas stop your husband and children join in the sorrow of our mutual loss stop letter follows love Doc* " (11.26). What everyone takes as mumbling is Holly remembering how Fred was the only one who let her snuggle close to him on cold nights, and she's grieving the loss of her brother.

Chapter 12

- Holly changes quite a bit after Fred's death. She doesn't talk about him anymore, she doesn't call the narrator Fred, and she hides out in her apartment for much of the summer. She also starts to even look very different. She stops dying her hair, she gains weight, and she stops caring about her clothes, even going "to the delicatessen wearing a rain-slicker and nothing underneath" (12.1). José moves in with Holly but he spends so much time in Washington that Holly is quite often alone.
- While this all sounds very sad, the narrator tells us that Holly "seem[s] more content, altogether happier than [he'd] ever seen her" (12.2). She develops an "un-Holly-like enthusiasm for homemaking" (12.2) and she starts buying furniture and cooking. She can't cook any regular dishes, but she can cook things like "brandied black terrapin poured into

avocado shells" and "roasted pheasant stuffed with pomegranates and persimmons" (12.2) (this suits her, don't you think?).

- Holly also starts talking about how things will be after she and José get married, even though José hasn't actually asked her to marry him and hasn't even mentioned getting married. But Holly assumes that this is the inevitable outcome since she's six weeks pregnant with José's child.
- Holly tells the narrator that she wants a big family, with nine kids, and that she "wish[es] [she'd] been a virgin for [José]. She tells him that she hasn't slept around as much as people assume she has and that she's "only had eleven lovers" (12.3). This doesn't include the people she slept with before she was thirteen but, according to Holly, "that just *doesn't* count" (12.3).
- She reveals to the narrator that José is not her perfect man – he bathes too much and is too loud when he eats, and he runs in a funny way, but she loves him and he can make her feel better when she has the mean reds (she doesn't even have to take Seconal or go to Tiffany's anymore).
- As summer turns into fall, Holly and the narrator spend a lot of time together, and their "understanding of each other […] reach[es] that sweet depth where two people communicate more often in silence than in words" (12.4).
- The narrator starts to "develop […] hostile attitudes toward *him*" (12.4) (he won't even say José's name anymore), and he and Holly spend their nights together when José is in Washington. One night, they're walking back home from Chinatown on the Brooklyn Bridge and Holly talks about bringing her kids back to New York: "Years from now, years and years, one of those ships will bring me back, me and my nine Brazilian brats. Because yes, they *must* see this, these lights, the river – I love New York, even though it isn't mine, the way something has to be, a tree or a street or a house, something, anyway, that belongs to me because I belong to it" (12.4).
- This makes the narrator very sad and he tells Holly to "shut up" (12.4), upset that he doesn't seem to be part of her future plans.

Chapter 13

- It's the narrator's birthday and he's waiting for the mail to come in the hopes that his family has sent him money. Holly happens to walk by and she invites him to go horseback riding in the park. Although she's pregnant and isn't "out to lose the heir" (13.2), she wants to say good-bye to a horse named Mabel.
- This is the first the narrator has heard of Holly leaving, and it turns out José has arranged for them to head to Brazil the following week. This news hits the narrator hard, and as they're on their way to the park, he feels like he's "flying, desolately floating over snow-peaked and perilous territory" (13.5). He tells Holly that she "can't *really* run off and leave everybody" (13.6). Holly tells him that no one will miss her, but he tells her that he'll miss her, and that Joe Bell and Sally Tomato will miss her too.
- It seems that Sally takes the news a little better than the narrator does, and he even tells Holly that she should go "because sooner or later there might be trouble" (13.9) (remember the "weather reports" she delivered to Sally? We're guessing it has something to do with

this). He even gives her five hundred bucks as a "wedding present" (13.9) (does this sound like a payoff to anyone else but us?).

- The narrator, clearly upset at the thought of Holly leaving, "want[s] to be unkind" (13.10), so he questions whether or not the wedding will actually happen and then brings up Holly's first husband, Doc. She warns him about telling anyone about Doc as she "rub[s] her nose" (13.15) (remember that she does this when she's getting upset or uncomfortable with a too-personal conversation).

- They finally get to the stables and mount their horses. Holly chooses one for the narrator that is "safer than a cradle" (13.16), and as they ride through Central Park the narrator starts to feel exhilarated and happy: "Suddenly, watching the tangled colors of Holly's hair flash in the red-yellow light, I loved her enough to forget myself, my self-pitying despairs, and be content that something she thought happy was going to happen" (13.18).

- As he's basking in these warm feelings and enjoying the horseback ride, a group of boys jump out of the bushes and scares his horse. The narrator reveals himself to be a bit of a racist (or at least to subscribe to some pretty racist stereotypes) when he describes the boys as a "band of Negro boys" (13.19) who act "like savage members of a jungle ambush" (13.19).

- The narrator's horse freaks out, stands on her hind legs (with him still on her), and then takes off running so fast that "her hooves made the gravel stones spit sparks" (13.20). Holly races after the narrator as his horse carries him to Fifth Avenue, "stampeding against the noon-day traffic, taxis, buses that screechingly swerved" (13.20). Holly keeps after them, and a policeman joins the chase as they maneuver their own horses on either side of the narrator's. This stops the horse suddenly and the narrator falls off, not really clear where he's ended up.

- After the policeman offers to take the horses back to the stables, Holly and the narrator get in a taxi and she is really, truly worried about him. "You might have been killed" (13.27), she tells him, her "face […] white with concern" (13.26). The narrator's a little embarrassed by the whole situation, but more than anything he's thankful that she stopped his horse: "But I wasn't. And thank you. For saving my life. You're wonderful. Unique. I love you" (13.28). Holly kisses the narrator's cheek when he says this, and then he promptly passes out.

Chapter 14

- This chapter is pretty short, but a whole lot happens in it. Pictures of Holly are in every major newspaper in the city that night because, shortly after getting back from the horseback ride, she's arrested for being part of a drug ring operated by Sally.

- The newspapers describe Holly as a "beautiful movie starlet and café society celebrity" (14.2), and they report her as a "*key figure*" (14.2) in Sally's drug operations. We also learn through the papers that the "lawyer" O'Shaughnessy is actually a " *defrocked priest*" (14.2) who's been in trouble with the law for years. He also gets arrested that night.

- So, it turns out the weather reports that Holly thought were just a way for O'Shaughnessy to make sure she had been to see Sally were actually "*verbally coded messages*" (14.2) that allowed Sally to "*keep first-hand control of a world-wide narcotics syndicate with*

outposts in Mexico, Cuba, Sicily, Tangier, Tehran and Dakar" (14.2).

- The newspapers are able to get a comment from Holly, and she freely admits to her weekly visits to Sing Sing. She defends Sally as a man who "*believes in God*" (14.2). She also admits to smoking marijuana from time to time, and the newspapers report this as Holly's admission of a drug addiction (which she very clearly did not actually admit).
- The newspapers also report that Holly got arrested in her apartment, but we learn from the narrator that she was actually arrested in his place, in his bathroom. Here's how it happens: After the horse-riding fiasco, the narrator is soaking in a bath while Holly keeps him company and waits to "rub him with Sloan's liniment and tuck [him] into bed" (14.3). They hear a knock at the door, and in bursts Madame Spanella (she's one of their neighbors who has never liked Holly and who tries to get her kicked out of the building at some point). Two detectives, "one of them a lady with thick yellow braids roped around her head" (14.3), follow her into the bathroom.
- Madame Spanella has always thought of Holly as a little too "easy," and when she sees Holly in the bathroom with the naked narrator (Holly is also naked for some reason that we're not sure of), she calls her a "'whore'" (14.4) and points her out to the detectives as "the wanted woman" (14.3).
- The male detective doesn't seem to know what to do with Holly, but the female detective displays a "harsh enjoyment" (14.4) as she physically tries to get Holly to come with them. Holly refuses and calls the woman a "dreary, driveling, old bull-dyke" (14.4). The female detective slaps Holly in the face, which makes her drop the glass bottle of liniment. This happens just as the narrator is trying to get out of the tub, and he steps on the broken glass, cuts his feet, and leaves blood all over the floor.
- As Holly is being taken away, she says one final thing to the narrator: "Don't forget, […] please feed the cat" (14.4) (so she does care about the nameless feline after all).

Chapter 15

- That night, Joe Bell shows up with the newspapers in hand, clearly freaking out about how much trouble Holly is in. He asks the narrator if he believes the stories about her, to which the narrator replies "yes," and this infuriates Joe (remember that the man's a little in love with Holly). The narrator clarifies that he doesn't think "she was involved *knowingly*" (15.4), but he reminds Joe that she did go visit Sally every week and that she did return with messages for O'Shaughnessy.
- Joe wants to find someone, anyone, to help Holly. He suggests that the narrator call Rusty Trawler, but the narrator refuses. He eventually calls O.J. Berman (the Hollywood agent from the beginning of the novel), but he can't get a hold of him. Joe keeps pressing the narrator to call Rusty, and when he finally does he ends up talking to Mag, who is less than sympathetic toward Holly: "My husband and I will positively *sue* anyone who attempts to connect our name with that ro-ro-ro*vol*ting and de-de-de*gen*erate girl" (15.8).
- The narrator realizes that Holly really doesn't have a lot of people in her life she can depend on, but he tries O.J. Berman one more time and finally gets in touch with him. It seems he's already heard about Holly's trouble and has hired the best lawyer in New York to defend her. He tells the narrator that Holly's bail will be posted and she'll get out

of jail that night.

Chapter 16

- It sounds like O.J. Berman has everything under control, but Holly doesn't actually get out of jail that first night. The narrator wants to feed her cat, but he has no key so he has to get into her apartment through the window.
- He finds the cat in Holly's bedroom, but he also finds a man in there who looks like José and who's packing up all of José's stuff. The narrator asks about José's whereabouts, but his cousin either isn't sure about this or just isn't willing to tell the narrator. He hands a letter to the narrator and asks that he give it to Holly on behalf of José. It's addressed very formally to "*Miss H. Golightly – Courtesy Bearer* (doesn't exactly sound like a passionate love letter, does it?).
- The narrator is so sad for Holly and he hugs the cat as he thinks about how crushed Holly will be when she realizes that José has left her.

Chapter 17

- The narrator is visiting Holly in a hospital room, where she's been kept since getting arrested. He doesn't want to tell her about José's letter, but he can't lie to her when she asks if he's heard from him. The narrator doesn't hand over the letter right away, and he and Holly instead start talking about why she's in the hospital.
- Holly tells the narrator that she's lost the baby, and this is when we hear about "the fat woman" (17.2) for the first time. Holly first sees this woman when Fred dies, and as she describes the lady to us and to the narrator, it becomes more clear that she's kind of a vision of death for Holly: "Right away I was wondering where he'd gone, what it meant, Fred dying; and then I saw her, she was there in the room with me, and she had Fred cradled in her arms, a fat mean red bitch rocking in a rocking chair with Fred on her lap and laughing like a brass band. The mockery of it! But it's all that's ahead for us, my friend: this comedienne waiting to give you the old razz" (17.2). It's the vision of this woman that makes Holly destroy everything in her apartment that night, and it's this same vision that haunts Holly when she first gets to the hospital. It seems that Holly was very close to dying as well.
- The narrator finally gives José's letter to Holly, but in true Holly form, she doesn't want to read it until she can apply her makeup. After putting on her makeup, donning her earrings, and putting on her dark glasses, she grabs the letter and reads it in the hopes of getting some good news. As we know, she does not.
- José tells Holly that he loves her but that he can't risk marrying a girl like her because of his political career. He tells her that he has "[his] family to protect, and [his] name, and [he is] a coward where those institutions enter" (17.8). He asks for her forgiveness, tells her that he's returned to Brazil, and tells her, "May God always be with you and your child" (17.8) (notice that he doesn't refer to the baby his child too).

- Holly is understandably angry, especially because she really "*did* love him. The rat" (17.13). And then we find out that the physical exertion from the disastrous horseback ride is what causes her to lose the baby. In order to scare the police department, she pretends that the slap from the female detective is the cause, and she tells the narrator that she might "sue them on several counts, including false arrest" (17.14).
- This is the first time Holly has mentioned the trouble she's in with the law, and the narrator is worried about her lack of plans. He wants to know what she is going to do to take care of things, and she tells him that she's still going to head to Brazil (not to follow José but because her ticket is already paid for – she might as well go).
- He reminds her that she can't just leave town while she's "under a criminal indictment" (17.21) since she'll either get caught and get thrown in jail for the rest of her life or she'll "never be able to come home" (17.21). Holly isn't at all concerned about getting caught, and she doesn't want to cooperate with the police since they want her to testify against Sally, which she absolutely will not do either. She tells him that she can't hang around New York anymore since she's sort of damaged goods (so she won't be able to make a living "off [her] particular talents" (17.24). And she refuses to sit around and watch Mag shop at Tiffany's with Rusty's money.
- Holly asks the narrator to go to her apartment and gather a few things for her trip, including the St. Christopher medal he gave her.

Chapter 18

- Holly continues to get ready for her trip, but the narrator has to do most of the preparation since the apartment is being watched at all times. When Holly gets out of the hospital, she firsts stops at the bank and then heads to Joe Bell's bar where she sends a message to the narrator to bring her guitar, her toothbrush, some brandy, and her cat. He does as she asks, packs up all the stuff she wants, and then treks to Joe's bar in the rain. It's a dreadful walk for him as the bags fall apart, he drops her perfume and some of her jewelry, and the cat scratches him.
- When he finally gets to the bar, Holly wants to toast with the brandy, but Joe wants no part of it. He's worried about Holly's escape plan and he doesn't want to celebrate what he thinks is a horrible, horrible mistake. But then a limo shows up and it turns out that Joe has hired the car to take Holly to the airport (he's really just a big softie). When she tries to thank him, Joe hands her some flowers, wishes her a quick good-bye, and hurries off.
- Holly and the narrator climb into the limo and head to the airport. When they reach a part of Spanish Harlem, Holly tells the driver to stop the limo, which he does. It's "a savage, a garish, a moody neighborhood garlanded with poster-portraits of movie stars and Madonnas. [And] Sidewalk litterings of fruit-rind and rotted newspaper were hurled about by the wind [...]" (18.11).
- Holly gets out of the car with the cat and tries to get him to run away: "This ought to be the right kind of place for a tough guy like you. Garbage cans. Rats galore. Plenty of cat-bums to gang around with. So scram" (18.12). The cat won't leave and instead looks at Holly as if he doesn't get what's going on. She tells him to "beat it!" (18. 12), but he still won't leave. So she finally yells at him, "I said fuck off!" (18.2), and then gets back in the limo and

tells the driver to drive.

- The narrator is "stunned" (18.13) by this and he tells Holly, "You *are* a bitch" (18.13). She tries to justify her actions by reminding him that she and the cat never belonged to each other, but even she isn't convinced by this, and when the limo stops at a red light she jumps out and tries to find the cat.
- She can't find the cat anywhere, so she and the narrator get back in the limo (he ran after her when she jumped out) and she finally admits that the cat really did belong to her: "Oh Jesus God. We did belong to each other. He was mine" (18.16). The narrator promises to find the cat and to take care of him, and this is when Holly finally admits that she's scared: "'But what about me?' she said, whispered, and shivered again. 'I'm very scared, Buster. Yes, at last. Because it could go on forever. Not knowing what's yours until you've thrown it away'" (18.18). As she gets ready to head to Brazil, Holly finally realizes that her life frightens her.

Chapter 19

- The newspapers start reporting Holly as missing (or even murdered), but then they eventually learn that she's in Rio. The police don't try to find her, and soon Holly isn't really big news anymore. No one hears from her from months and the apartment owner sells all of her stuff and rents her apartment to a new guy who "entertained as many gentleman callers of a noisy nature as Holly ever had" (19.1).
- The narrator finally gets a postcard from Holly, who tells him that she's made her way to Buenos Aires, that she's fallen in love with a married man who has seven kids, and that she doesn't have an address yet but she'll send it when she gets one.
- The narrator never hears from her after this, and this saddens him since "there [is] so much he want[s] to write her" (19.1). He wants to tell her about the stories he's sold, about Mag and Rusty's nasty divorce, about moving out of the apartment "because it was haunted" (19.1). And he wants to tell her that he did find her cat after searching and searching. On "one cold sun-shiny Sunday winter afternoon" (19.1), he sees the cat "in the window of a warm-looking room" (19.1). He wants to know what the cat's name is since he's "certain he ha[s] one now" (19.1), and he's also "certain he'[s] arrived somewhere he [belongs]" (19.1).
- The narrator's final thought is about Holly, and he hopes that she has found the place where she belongs as well.

Themes

Theme of Isolation

Isolation, the desire for it, and the fear of it, are central themes in *Breakfast at Tiffany's* . In many ways, isolation reflects a desire to remain unconfined by close personal relationships since a life spent alone presents no complicated attachments to other people. But too much

isolation also proves to be a source of great fear as characters realize that we all desire a sense of belonging at some point in our lives. We see isolation propel some characters and we see it prevent others from ever moving forward in their lives, and it impacts most aspects of the novel.

Questions About Isolation

1. Is Holly's isolation somehow different from that of the other characters?
2. Is the narrator isolated in some way?
3. Does isolation automatically equate to loneliness for the characters?

Chew on Isolation

Isolation is a destructive force since it prevents the development of true connections between characters.

Isolation actually protects certain characters since it keeps them from getting hurt. It's when they relinquish isolation that they experience pain.

Theme of Friendship

Friendship is a complicated thing. It can be wonderful and fulfilling and it can also be painful and devastating. The friendships in this novel are, for the most part, superficial and are often based on what one person can get from another. But every once in a while true friendship develops and we notice this even more because of how anomalous it is. These friendships represent the particularly interesting relationships in *Breakfast at Tiffany's* because they allow us to see instances of loyalty, tenderness, and caring in the midst of a world that seems to be lacking these things.

Questions About Friendship

1. Are Holly and the narrator really friends by the end of the novel?
2. Do Holly's friends function as her family, in some way?
3. Does friendship depend on a sense of loyalty in the novel?

Chew on Friendship

We never see an instance of true friendship in the novel. Most of the characters just want something from their so-called friends.

Joe Bell, the narrator, and O.J. Berman display actual qualities of a friend when it comes to Holly.

Theme of Dreams, Hopes, and Plans

On a basic level, *Breakfast at Tiffany's* is about looking forward to the future and about the dreams, hopes, and plans we make for ourselves. In many ways these dreams sustain the characters, as they are propelled by the promise of something better than what the present can provide. But when these same hopes, and plans are shattered, this has devastating effects on the dreamers. Suddenly, they have to revise what they've been looking forward to, and this throws some characters into a tailspin as they're suddenly forced to reevaluate their lives.

Questions About Dreams, Hopes, and Plans

1. Do the characters suffer because of their dreams, hopes, and plans?
2. Is Holly the only character who actually has a plan?
3. Does the narrator's dream of being a writer influence our reading of the story? If so, how?

Chew on Dreams, Hopes, and Plans

The dreams and plans the characters have are pipe dreams. They'll never actually see these aspirations come to be.

None of the characters actually have any plans. They just float through life waiting to see what happens.

Theme of Memory and the Past

Memory and the past are both positive and negative forces in *Breakfast at Tiffany's* . For some characters, memories are the only truly happy things they have in their lives since those recollections represent a simpler and safer time. But, in other instances, memories and the past simply won't let go of their hold on the characters' lives and those people are forced to face them again and again. These memories become harmful or sad when characters can't move past them or can't look beyond them to the hope of finding happiness in the present and in the future.

Questions About Memory and the Past

1. Do Holly's memories of Fred prevent her from moving forward in her life?
2. What does it mean when the narrator tells us that the brownstone is "haunted" after Holly's departure?
3. Can the characters ever escape their pasts?

Chew on Memory and the Past

Breakfast at Tiffany's is an exercise in looking back. It's all about how the past sustains the characters.

The novel is about leaving the past behind and looking forward to better things in the future.

Theme of Transience

The idea of transience informs nearly every aspect of *Breakfast at Tiffany's* . It's the desire to remain unfettered and unchained that propels Holly and that drives much of the action of the story, and there's a definite sense of impermanence throughout the narrative. We get the feeling early on that the relationships and connections that develop won't be long-lasting, that they are matters of convenience more than anything else. And this take on relationships creates a general feeling of anxiety since we're always waiting for the other shoe to drop. In a world marked by transience, it's hard to know what to hold onto (both for the characters and for us as readers), and this impacts how we read the novel since it puts us on edge.

Questions About Transience

1. Is the presence of transience somehow the result of World War II?
2. Would the sense of impermanence be different if the novel was set in a rural setting instead of an urban setting?
3. Is transience different for the male characters than it is for the female characters?

Chew on Transience

The idea of transience applies just to the physical settings in the novel.

Transience operates on a symbolic level. It's indicative of a larger, metaphorical theme in the novel.

Theme of Freedom and Confinement

The desire for freedom and the fear of confinement are in keeping with the other themes in *Breakfast at Tiffany's* . The need for freedom compels characters to act in strange ways in order to protect their independence, and they react just as strongly when they experience an impending sense of confinement. The desire for freedom also prevents some characters from allowing others to get too close, for fear that these others will then have some power over them. Some characters can't even look at literal tools of confinement like cages because of what these things represent.

Questions About Freedom and Confinement

1. Does Holly suffer from too much freedom?
2. Is the narrator somehow confined?
3. Is it possible that Holly actually craves confinement in some way?

Chew on Freedom and Confinement

There's no such thing as freedom in the novel. We just see the illusion of freedom.

The characters in the novel are truly free since most of them are unencumbered by concerns about other people. Their self-involvement represents true freedom.

Theme of The Home

There's no single idea of "home" in *Breakfast at Tiffany's* , and this is what makes it such an interesting theme. For some, home is a feeling of belonging, and it doesn't matter where this is. For others, home has to do with the people who surround them and who make them feel safe. Home is not just the literal place where one lives. It's not the apartment or house that gives someone an address. It might be an entire city or the feeling of being near family, and it means different things to different people depending on their life experiences.

Questions About The Home

1. Do you think it's possible for Holly to ever find a true home? Why or why not?
2. Does the novel challenge traditional ideas of home or does it somehow reinforce them?
3. Does the brownstone apartment building really feel like home to any of its tenants?

Chew on The Home

Home for these characters is the whole city of New York. It's the sights and sounds of this specific place that make them feel at home.

The idea of home is symbolic. For Holly, home is where the heart is.

Theme of Love

We get a just a few direct mentions of "love" in *Breakfast at Tiffany's* , but it's still pretty important because we are presented with a lot of different ideas about what love really is. There are instances of unconditional love, unrequited love, love between friends, and love in the more traditional sense. And, at some point in the novel, each of these types of love result in pain and sadness. There is no fairy-tale love in this story. Instead, we get a more realistic picture of love – complicated, messy, and sometimes extremely painful.

Questions About Love

1. Do you think Holly falls in love with the narrator at all?
2. Does one character best represent the idea of love?
3. Is Holly's cat the only one who really loves her?

Chew on Love

The characters who fall in love with Holly just fall in love with the idea of her. It's not the real Holly they love.

Joe Bell, Doc, and the narrator really love Holly. In fact, they love her in spite of the persona she constructs for herself.

Quotes

Isolation Quotes

Like many people with a bold fondness for volunteering personal information, anything that suggested a direct question, a pinning-down, put her on guard (3.23).

Thought: Holly's unwillingness to answer direct questions reflects her active move to isolate herself from other people. This way she's always in control.

Her cheek came to rest against my shoulder, a warm damp weight. "Why are you crying?" She sprang back, sat up. "Oh, for God's sake," she said, starting for the window and the fire escape, "I hate snoops" (3.58).

Thought: There's a brief moment when Holly lets down her guard and invites someone in, but as soon as the narrator presses her she goes back to isolating herself.

"We sort of just took up by the river one day, we don't belong to each other: he's an independent and, so am I" (4.52).

Thought: Holly won't even allow herself to form ties with a cat. She remains completely isolated from anything that could represent personal attachment.

She talked of her own [childhood], too; but it was elusive, nameless, placeless, an impressionistic recital (7.2).

Thought: One of the ways Holly maintains her isolation is by only offering up generalities about herself. She appears to share some personal information, but it's too non-descript to really mean anything.

We wore the masks all the way home (7.6).

Thought: This is the scene when Holly and the narrator steal the Halloween masks from Woolworth's, and it carries a great deal of symbolic meaning in relation to the idea of isolation. There are a lot of masks Holly hides behind, and this allows her to maintain the isolation she seems to need so dearly.

I stepped on Holly's dark glasses, they were lying on the floor, the lenses already shattered, the frames cracked in half (11.8).

Thought: This occurs after Holly finds out about Fred's death, and the smashed glasses show us that she can't maintain total isolation from the people around her. What were once the symbol of her isolation – her glasses – have been destroyed when the narrator sees how profoundly impacted Holly is by the loss of her brother.

"I told you. We just met by the river one day: that's all. Independents, both of us. We never made each other any promises. We never – " she said, and her voiced collapsed [...] (18.14).

Thought: After Holly turns her cat loose, she tries to convince herself that she's happy being alone, but we see that this really isn't the case.

"Dead. Or in a crazy house. Or married. I think she's married and quieted down and maybe right in this very city" (1.31).

Thought: This is the narrator's answer to Joe's question about Holly's whereabouts, and it's pretty significant that his first instinct is to think that she's dead or locked away somewhere. It seems she's been rather successful in convincing the world that she is meant to spend her life alone.

Only: what other friends of hers did I know? Perhaps she'd been right when she said she had none, not really (15.7).

Thought: The narrator thinks this after Holly's arrest when he can't get a hold of anyone to help her. He realizes that her isolation is so complete that only he and Joe are concerned about her well-being. This is one negative consequence of her isolation.

"My husband and I will positively sue anyone who attempts to connect our names with that ro-ro-rovolting and de-de-degenerate girl" (15.8).

Thought: This is Mag's reaction to hearing from the narrator after Holly's arrest. We can't really blame her for not wanting to help Holly since the woman did steal her fiancée, but this does show us the consequences of Holly's behavior. Part of her isolation stems from a lack of care with other people's feelings, and this results in anger and bitterness from those affected.

Friendship Quotes

"[...] our understanding of each other had reached that sweet depth where two people communicate more often in silence than in words" (12.4).

Thought: This makes us believe that perhaps Holly and the narrator really do develop a true friendship. They reach a level of comfort that only true friends achieve.

"No, idiot. This is serious. Look at me. [...] You might have been killed" (13.25-13.27).

Thought: After the horseback-riding fiasco, Holly displays real tenderness and concern for the narrator – she actually cares for him. And this is a touching moment between the two that shows us that Holly is indeed capable of friendship.

"It makes me furious, the way these wretched people keep persecuting him. He's a sensitive, a religious person. A darling old man" (14.2).

Thought: Even after Holly is arrested for associating with Sally Tomato, she refuses to believe that he's the horrible man the newspapers are making him out to be. Is she being naïve? Perhaps. But she might also just be displaying the loyalty she feels toward the people she believes are her friends.

"Boy, that's rotten. And you meant to be her friend. What a bastard!" (15.4).

Thought: This reveals to us Joe Bell's definition of friendship. He is appalled that the narrator thinks Holly is really involved in the mess with Sally Tomato. For Joe, true friendship is the complete belief in a friend's innocence.

"Well, I might be rotten to the core, Maude, but: testify against a friend I will not" (17.24).

Thought: So, Holly actually does think about someone other than herself. For her, friendship cannot exist without loyalty (even if we think her loyalty might be a little misguided in this case.

But the address, if it ever existed, never was sent, which made me sad, there was so much I wanted to write her (19.1).

Thought: In the end, the narrator just misses his friend a great deal. He wants to share the accomplishments of his life with her, and he feels her absence in a very real way.

I had kept my promise; I had found him (19.1).

Thought: Although he doesn't have to do this, the narrator keeps his word to Holly and finds her cat. It seems he feels that loyalty is a part of friendship, too.

"I don't think anyone will miss me. I have no friends" (13.7).

Thought: Is this Holly feeling sorry for herself or is she just speaking the truth? Either way, she seems a bit saddened by this realization and we get to see a crack in her armor.

"But there's a horse, my darling old Mabel Minerva – I can't go without saying good-bye to Mabel Minerva" (13.2).

Thought: It's much easier for Holly to form attachments to animals than to people. This horse is her friend, a thing she loves and holds dear to her heart.

"But Holly! It's dreadful!" "I couldn't agree more; but I thought you wanted it" (8.6-8.7).

Thought: Although Holly doesn't like the idea of the birdcage, she buys it for the narrator because she thinks it will make him happy. She is capable of self-sacrifice when it comes to the people she really cares about.

Dreams, Hopes, and Plans Quotes

"She had something working for her, she had them interested, she could've really rolled. But when you walk out on a thing like that, you don't walk back" (4.18).

Thought: O.J. Berman can't understand how Holly could simply walk away from the chance to make it in Hollywood. For him, this signifies her inability to plan or her lack of thoughts about her future.

"If I do feel guilty, I guess it's because I let him go on dreaming when I wasn't dreaming a bit" (4.51).

Thought: This is Holly's take on why she didn't pursue her Hollywood career. It's not that she wasn't thinking about her future; she just knew that being in Hollywood wasn't her dream – it was O.J.'s dream for her.

"Every day she'd walk a little further: a mile, come home. Two miles, and come home. One day she just kept on" (9.18).

Thought: When Holly leaves Tulip, Texas, it's a decision she makes without much planning. She knows there is something more for her out in the world. So, although she's not sure what her plans are once she leaves Doc, she hopes she'll find a different life.

"Good luck: and believe me, dearest Doc – it's better to look at the sky than live here. Such an empty place; so vague" (10.11).

Thought: It seems New York is a difficult place to make definite plans. The emptiness and the vagueness of the city make it hard to hold on to something concrete, to hope for something specific.

"I don't want to own anything until I know I've found the place where me and things belong to each other. I'm not quite sure where that is just yet. But I know what it's like" (4.52).

Thought: This is Holly's big hope for her life – to find a place where she feels she belongs. She doesn't know where this place is, but she's confident it's out there and she knows how she'll feel when she finds it.

Her bedroom was consistent with her parlor: it perpetuated the same camping-out atmosphere; crates and suitcases, everything packed and ready to go (6.3).

Thought: Holly's apartment speaks to her lack of plans. She lives an impetuous life and it seems she's always ready to go where the wind may take her.

When she'd left, I wandered over to the table where her books remained; they were what I had wanted to see. South by Thunderbird. Byways of Brazil. The Political Mind of South America. And so forth.

Thought: These books reveal one of Holly's more underhanded plans. She's educating herself about José's world, perhaps so she can become a part of it. It seems she can make plans when they'll benefit her.

"He'll marry me, all right. In church. And with his family there" (13.11).

Thought: Holly has actually allowed herself to dream of a more secure life with José. She's finally looking forward to the future and she feels confident that her dreams will come true this time. She's supremely confident in the plans she has for her life.

"Years from now, years and years, one of those ships will bring me back, me and my nine Brazilian brats" (12.4).

Thought: In a rare moment, Holly pictures herself as an older woman with a family. She imagines that she and José will have a big family and that she'll spend the rest of her life in Brazil. She's looking beyond the immediate future here and is daring to plan for years and years to come.

"Today's Wednesday, isn't it? So I suppose I'll sleep until Saturday, really get a good schluffen. Saturday morning I'll skip out to the bank. Then I'll stop by the apartment and pick up a nightgown or two and my Mainbocher. Following which, I'll report to Idlewild. Where, as you damn well know, I have a perfectly fine reservation on a perfectly fine plane" (17.18).

Thought: It's so easy for Holly to slip back into her old habits. After José dashes her hopes of marriage and a family, Holly resorts to what's familiar to her – living life on the fly and living for the moment.

Memory and the Past Quotes

"Like my brother Fred. We used to sleep four in a bed, and he was the only one that ever let me hug him on a cold night" (3.7).

Thought: Memories of Fred represent happy recollections of Holly's past. In the midst of her difficult childhood, her brother was a source of safety and security.

I am always drawn back to places where I have lived, the houses and their neighborhoods (1.1).

Thought: These words open the novel and let us know that we'll be spending time in the past. The story is framed around the idea of looking back.

"You take a man that likes to walk, a man like me, a man's been walking in the streets going on ten or twelve years, and all those years he's got his eye out for one person, and nobody's ever her, don't it stand to reason she's not there" (1.32).

Thought: Joe Bell desperately wants to recapture the past, to go back to the chapter when Holly was in his life. He spends his days looking for the woman who can carry him back to a different time.

"She's such a goddamn liar, maybe she don't know herself any more" (4.20).

Thought: Holly has spent so much time trying to leave behind Lulamae Barnes that it's possible she doesn't really know who she is – Holiday or Lulamae or anything else. This passage reveals Holly's deep desire to erase the past.

"Even though I kept telling him: But Doc, I'm not fourteen any more, and I'm not Lulamae. But the terrible part is (and I realized it while we were standing there) I am. I'm still stealing turkey eggs and running through a brier patch. Only now I call it having the mean reds" (11.5).

Thought: Despite her best efforts, Holly can't escape her past. A part of her will always be Lulamae Barnes from Texas.

"He's the only one would ever let me. Let me hug him on cold nights. I saw a place in Mexico. With horses. By the sea" (11.10).

Thought: When Holly's ties to the happy parts of her past disappear, it destroys her. Fred was her one constant link to a past she remembered fondly, and his death erases that for her in an instant.

A disquieting loneliness came into my life, but it induced no hunger for friends of longer acquaintance: they seemed now like a salt-free, sugarless diet (4.1).

Thought: The narrator's present is more exciting now that Holly's a part of it. His past no longer holds the pull it once did.

"She's strictly a girl you'll read where she ends up at the bottom of a bottle of Seconals. I've seen it happen more times than you've got toes" (4.16).

Thought: Although this is O.J.'s prediction for Holly's future, it has everything to do with her past. He believes her eventual fate will come as the result of all of her prior, very bad decisions.

So the days, the last days, blow about in memory, hazy, autumnal, all alike as leaves: until a day unlike any other I've lived (12.5).

Thought: The narrator's memories of his last few days with Holly fade into an indefinite picture because he's so sad at the thought of her leaving. He knows she's going to become a part of his past, not a part of his future.

[I] was moving out of the brownstone because it was haunted (19.1).

Thought: The narrator can't escape memories of Holly once she has left, and he can't bear to stay in the apartment since it's a constant reminder of her. He has to remove himself from the physical location of his memories in order to move on.

Transience Quotes

"I'm very scared, Buster. Yes, at last. Because it could go on forever. Not knowing what's yours until you've thrown it away" (18.18).

Thought: Holly has spent her life avoiding anything permanent, but as she heads to the airport she finally admits that this impermanence scares her because she sees no end to it. The idea of transience stretches before her indefinitely.

"I don't. I'll never get used to anything. Anybody that does, they might as well be dead" (3.12).

Thought: The idea of staying put feels like a death sentence for Holly. To her, life is about continuing to move and to experience new things. She doesn't believe in staying in one place long enough to get used to it.

I wondered if she'd often stolen. "I used to," she said. "I mean I had to. If I wanted anything. But I still do it every now and then, sort of to keep my hand in" (7.5).

Thought: A part of Holly knows that she might have to pick up and go at any moment, and she expects that she might have to struggle to survive. Living her life on the fly permanently affects her day-to-day actions.

She was forever on her way out [...] (8.2).

Thought: This short passage perfectly sums up Holly's life. She's always on the move, always onto something better.

Holly was not a girl who could keep anything, and surely by now she had lost that medal, left it in a suitcase or some hotel drawer (8.10).

Thought: The narrator doesn't count on Holly hanging on to the St. Christopher medal he gives her for Christmas, and this shows us that nothing in Holly's life is permanent. It's not just her geographical location that changes, and it's not just the people who float in and out of her life – she doesn't even hold tight to the sentimental gifts she receives.

One went: Don't wanna sleep, Don't wanna die, Just wanna go a-travelin' through the pastures of the sky; and this one seemed to gratify her the most [...] (3.5).

Thought: This is one of the songs Holly often sings when she's waiting for her hair to dry. It's pretty significant that it's one of her favorites since it's all about the desire to keep moving, to keep traveling. The singer wants nothing as permanent as sleep or death.

Everything was piled on the floor of my room, a poignant pyramid of brassieres and dancing slippers and pretty things I packed in Holly's only suitcase. There was a mass left over that I had to put in paper grocery bags (18.3).

Thought: It just seems kind of fitting that Holly's belongings have to be stuffed in disposable luggage. Even her bags are transient, impermanent.

She hummed to herself, swigged brandy, she leaned constantly forward to peer out the windows, as if she were hunting an address – or, I decided, taking a last impression of a scene she wanted to remember. It was neither of these (18.11).

Thought: The narrator wants to believe that Holly wishes to solidify her memories before leaving for Brazil, but this is his desire, not hers. Fixed memories would signify something too permanent for Holly, and this just isn't who she is.

The owner of the brownstone sold her abandoned possessions, the white-satin bed, the tapestry, her precious Gothic chair (19.1).

Thought: Holly leaves so most of her (already few) belongings behind when she escapes to South America. She's unencumbered by possessions, and even the things that would suggest a degree of permanence in her life get sold. Her consistent lack of furniture, and of "things" in general, symbolize the transience of her life.

"Then nothing," he shrugged. "By and by she went like she come, rode away on a horse" (1.26).

Thought: This is the end of Joe's story about Holly in Africa, but it's in the beginning pages of the novel itself. This passage prepares us for the transience that characterizes Holly for the rest of the narrative. She just comes and goes in Joe's story, just as she does in Capote's.

Freedom and Confinement Quotes

Afterwards, avoiding the zoo (Holly said she couldn't bear to see anything in a cage), we giggled, ran, sang along the paths toward the old wooden boathouse, now gone (7.2).

Thought: Holly's resistance to being confined extends beyond people to include animals as well. While some may see the zoo as a place to learn and interact, Holly sees it as a prison.

It was near the antique shop with the palace of a bird cage in its window, so I took her there to see it, and she enjoyed the point, its fantasy: "But still, it's a cage" (7.4).

Thought: Although this passage is similar to the one about the zoo, we think the birdcage is such a significant symbol that it's worth mentioning. Holly can appreciate the beauty of the cage, but she can't get in line with what it stands for.

"Bless you, Buster. And bless you for being such a bad jockey. If I hadn't had to play Calamity Jane I'd still be looking forward to the grub in an unwed mama's home" (17.14).

Thought: Holly loses her baby after rescuing the narrator from his out-of-control horse, and she pretends to be happy that she'll be free from motherhood. But we know this is just an act. She seems genuinely happy when she's pregnant, suggesting that being a mother doesn't signify confinement to her.

Holly stepped out of the car; she took the cat with her. Cradling him, she scratched his head and asked, "What do you think? This ought to be the right kind of place for a tough guy like you. […] So scram," she said, dropping him (18.12).

Thought: Holly's poor cat. She knows she loves him and we know she loves him, but he represents being tied down to something, and Holly just isn't prepared to do this yet. This innocent cat signifies confinement to skittish Holly.

Brazil was beastly but Buenos Aires the best. Not Tiffany's, but almost (19.1).

Thought: Holly's postcard tells us that she has secured her literal freedom in that she has escaped the authorities and is living her life in South America. But she still hasn't found her Tiffany's quite yet.

"Look. Don't despise me, darling." She put her hand over mine and pressed it with sudden immense sincerity. "I haven't much choice […]" (17.24).

Thought: After spending her life cultivating freedom and resisting confinement, Holly finds herself left with little actual freedom when it comes to her future. She doesn't have many options after being arrested so, in the end, she's pretty confined by the decisions she's made.

"And if you lived off my particular talents, Cookie, you'd understand the kind of bankruptcy I'm describing" (17.24).

Thought: Holly has painted herself into a corner, so to speak. She can't stay in New York because she has no way to make any money after she gets arrested. The places she used to visit and the people she used to depend on just won't welcome her anymore, so her future has been decided for her. She has no real freedom when it comes down to it.

"Can't you see that Rusty feels safer in diapers than he would in a skirt? Which is really the choice, only he's awfully touchy about it. He tried to stab me with a butter knife because I told him to grow up and face the issue, settle down and play house with a nice fatherly truck driver" (4.72).

Thought: Holly believes in everyone's absolute freedom to live their lives in ways that make them happy, and this includes the freedom to be honest about one's sexual preference. But Rusty clearly doesn't feel free enough to admit that he's gay.

"She believes all this crap she believes. You can't talk her out of it" (4.16).

Thought: Holly feels absolutely secure in the freedom to believe in whatever she wants. She simply won't be confined by other people's expectations of what's right or normal or good.

Holly suggested she run out to Woolworth's and steal some balloons; she did: and they turned the tree into a fairly good show (8.4).

Thought: We're not condoning stealing here, but in some ways the act of stealing represents freedom for Holly. She doesn't have to steal, but she still does because she can. She's just exercising her right to do what she wants, legal or not.

The Home Quotes

Even so, whenever I felt in my pocket the key to this apartment; with all its gloom, it still was a place of my own, the first, and my books were there, and jars of pencils to sharpen, everything I needed, so I felt, to become the writer I wanted to be (1.1).

Thought: Even though his apartment is small, old, and dingy the narrator loves it because it's his. This apartment is home to him because it represents the start of his career as a writer and the beginning of life on his own.

"Oh, you get used to anything," I said, annoyed with myself, for actually I was proud of the place (3.11).

Thought: After Holly criticizes the narrator's apartment and he agrees with her in order to save face, he feels like he's betrayed his home since it's a place he actually loves a lot. This passage presents us with the interesting idea that betrayal can extend to an idea like "the home."

"If I could find a real-life place that made me feel like Tiffany's, then I'd buy some furniture and give the cat a name. I've thought maybe after the war, Fred and I – " (4.58).

Thought: This is Holly's idea of home in a nutshell. It needs to be a place where she feels safe and it needs to include Fred. Home is both the place where she feels secure and is the people who she surrounds herself with.

I warmed to the room at once, I liked its fly-by-night look (4.4).

Thought: The narrator finds the unlived-in quality of Holly's apartment very appealing. It's the lack of a homey feeling that he's actually drawn to.

"If only I could get used to the idea of m-m-marrying a Brazilian. And being a B-b-brazilian myself. It's such a canyon to cross. Six thousand miles, and not knowing the language – " *(5.16).*

Thought: As Mag gets ready to move to Brazil with José, she laments the fact that she has to leave America. To her, the idea of home is very much tied to one's nationality and to one's physical location.

That Monday in October, 1943. A beautiful day with the buoyancy of a bird. To start, we had Manhattans at Joe Bell's; and, when he heard of my good luck, champagne cocktails on the house. Later, we wandered toward Fifth Avenue, where there was a parade. The flags in the wind, the thump of military bands and military feet, seemed to have nothing to do with war, but to be, rather, a fanfare arranged in my personal honor (7.1).

Thought: OK, bear with us. After getting his first story published, the narrator feels like New York is rolling out its best for him. The city, and the people and sights that are a part of it, are at this moment his happy home.

"She had good cause to run off from that house. She didn't have none to leave mine. 'Twas her home" (9.18).

Thought: Doc's idea of home is simple and humble. In his eyes, Holly had all the home she needed with him as his wife and as the stepmother of his children. He just doesn't get the idea of leaving a home like his to search for something different.

"Anyway, home is where you feel at home. I'm still looking" (17.22).

Thought: We couldn't ask for a more perfect articulation of Holly's idea of home. It's not a place but a feeling, not a physical location but an emotional reaction.

Flanked by potted plants and framed by clean lace curtains, he was seated in the window of a warm-looking room: I wondered what his name was, for I was certain he had one now, certain he'd arrived somewhere he belonged (19.1).

Thought: Holly's cat finally finds a home in his owner's absence, and the narrator knows it's a home because someone cares enough to give him a name and to claim him. The cat finally belongs to someone, and this is what makes this place home.

African hut or whatever, I hope Holly has, too (19.1).

Thought: This is the narrator's final wish for Holly – that she finds a place that feels like home no matter where it is or what it looks like. He wants her to feel the sense of belonging that her cat finally gets to experience.

Love Quotes

"Sure I loved her. But it wasn't that I wanted to touch her" (1.35).

Thought: Joe loves Holly in a way that doesn't require sex. He loves her without it being about a physical relationship. He loves her just for her.

"You can love somebody without it being like that. You keep them a stranger, a stranger who's a friend" (1.35).

Thought: This is yet another iteration of love from Joe and it reveals the possibility of loving someone who we never really know. Holly is not a stranger to Joe in the literal sense, but she's a stranger in the sense that he doesn't know much about her. Even so, he can still love her from afar. He can still love her as one friend would another.

"Of course he was never my lover; as far as that goes, I never knew him until he was already in jail. But I adore him now, after all I've been going to see him every Thursday for seven months, and I think I'd go even if he didn't pay me" (3.40).

Thought: Holly doesn't love Sally in the traditional sense, but she has come to feel great affection for the man over the past seven months of their relationship. Her love for him is like a granddaughter for her grandfather. She adores him more than anything else.

She sighed and picked up her knitting. "I must be madly in love. You saw us together. Do you think I'm madly in love?" (5.18).

Thought: Mag's love for José is not something she's confident in or sure about. She needs reassurance from Holly that she's actually in love, which tells us that maybe she doesn't really love José after all. Is true love something we have to convince ourselves of?

"Doc really loves me, you know. And I love him. He may have looked old and tacky to you. But you don't know the sweetness if him, the confidence he can give to birds and brats and fragile things like that. Anyone who ever gave you confidence, you owe them a lot" (10.3).

Thought: Holly's love for Doc is pretty complicated. On the one hand, it's kind of selfish on Holly's part because Doc makes her feel better about herself. But she's also very giving, in a way, because she feels indebted to Doc for all he's done for her. This love is about the give and take between a couple.

For I was in love with her. Just as I'd once been in love with my mother's elderly colored cook and a postman who let me follow him on his rounds and a whole family named McKendrick. That category of love generates jealousy, too (11.1).

Thought: The narrator's love for Holly is hard to pin down. He likens it to the other times in his life when he has felt great affection for people who were kind to him. But he also admits to feeling jealous when it comes to Holly, and this suggests there's indeed something more than affection going on. He is in love with her – he doesn't just love her.

I wish, please don't laugh – but I wish I'd been a virgin for him, for José (12.3).

Thought: This is an interesting statement coming from Holly since she seems so indifferent to what people consider acceptable. But she reveals herself to be a bit of a traditionalist here. And she also exposes the desire to change part of her past in order to please the man she loves, which is very unlike her.

"A person ought to be able to marry men or women or – listen, if you came to me and said you wanted to hitch up with Man o' War, I'd respect your feeling. No, I'm serious. Love should be allowed. I'm all for it" (12.3).

Thought: Holly believes in love without restrictions or rules. She truly feels that everyone should be free to pursue the love that makes them happy.

I loved her enough to forget myself, my self-pitying despairs, and be content that something she thought happy was going to happen (13.18).

Thought: The narrator's love for Holly reaches the point where it's no longer about his happiness – it becomes about her happiness even more. He finds contentment in the thought that she'll finally find security and stability.

"But oh gee, golly goddamn," she said, jamming a fist into her mouth like a bawling baby, "I did love him. The rat" (17.13).

Thought: Love can also mean pain. Holly finally let her guard down, finally let herself fall in love with someone. But when José leaves her, the loss of his love thrusts her right back into her old life and her former ways.

Plot Analysis

Classic Plot Analysis

Initial Situation
Holly and the narrator meet.
This meeting sets off the action in the rest of the novel, and the relationship between the two profoundly affects the narrator's life. It's also through the narrator's eyes that we get to know Holly, so it's pretty important that the two become acquainted.

Conflict
Holly and the narrator have an argument on Christmas Eve.
The narrator realizes that he and Holly are on totally different wavelengths. She criticizes the things he writes about (and completely misunderstands them), and he just doesn't get the choices she makes. After the narrator insults her intelligence and wants to hit her, Holly throws him out of her apartment. The narrator vows never to talk to her again.

Complication
Doc Golightly shows up in New York.
The narrator is still angry with Holly, but he notices a strange man watching her apartment and feels compelled to warn her about him. We learn that this man is Holly's husband and that she married him when she was just fourteen years old. He relates the sad story of her childhood and this complicates the narrator's perception of Holly (and ours, too).

Climax
Holly has an affair with José, gets pregnant, and plans to move to Brazil with him.
There are quite a few climactic moments in the novel, but this one is pretty big since it represents the big break between Holly and the narrator and Holly and New York (the city she

loves). Once she has decided to leave, the narrator is forced to think about what his life will be like without her, and he also admits that he's a little in love with Holly. Everything changes from this point on, which is why we think it's the climax of the story.

Suspense

Holly gets arrested for her part in Sally Tomato's drug ring.

Holly's arrest totally interrupts her plans and we're left in major suspense about her fate. Will she go to jail? Will she make it to Brazil? Will she admit to knowing about what Sally was really up to? We don't know what's going to happen to her, and this is the first time in the novel that Holly seems like she's in a situation she won't be able to charm her way out of.

Denouement

José leaves Holly and she also loses the baby.

Now that Holly knows she's not going to live happily ever after with José and their baby, she starts to make some definite decisions about her future (sort of). She prepares to skip town, to leave behind the narrator and Joe Bell and the mess with Sally Tomato, and she starts to wind down her time in New York City (while finally admitting that she's scared of continuing her life as it has been). This would seem like the conclusion, yet there's still more to come.

Conclusion

Holly leaves New York and the narrator gets a postcard from her.

The conclusion is pretty open-ended, so we can't really say for sure what happens to Holly once and for all. But she does leave New York and we do know that she has made it to South America, so in terms of the actual plot, this signifies the end of the story's action. The postcard lets us know that she's no longer living in the brownstone, no longer hanging out with the narrator, and no longer socializing in the same circles.

Booker's Seven Basic Plots Analysis: The Quest

The Call

Holly leaves Texas, Doc Golightly, and his kids and heads to New York

Holly realizes that there's more to see in the world than Tulip, Texas, and she sets out to live her life, to have some adventures, and to enjoy being young. Although Booker tells us that the hero "is given supernatural and visionary direction as to the distant, life-renewing goal he must aim for," and although it becomes clear pretty early on that Holly has no such direction, she still recognizes the call of something better and she answers that call.

The Journey

Holly's life in New York until she meets José

OK, bear with us on this one. Most of Holly's life in New York represents her journey to find the happiness she's looking for, so it's hard for us to choose just one scene that represents this stage. Her relationships with various (and creepy) men, her brush with Hollywood stardom, her relationship with Rusty Trawler, her involvement with Sally Tomato, and her friendship with the narrator all lead up to her eventual desire for a settled life, so we think these are all part of the journey stage.

Arrival and Frustration
Holly gets pregnant and wants to marry José
At some point, Holly realizes that what she wants is a settled life. She seems really happy taking care of José and she can imagine her life as his wife. But for a long time José doesn't propose and doesn't even mention the idea of marriage, so Holly is initially frustrated in her attempts to create that life for herself.

The Final Ordeals
José proposes, Holly gets arrested, and José leaves
José eventually proposes and it seems that Holly is close to finally getting what she wants. But when she gets arrested and José leaves her because of the resulting scandal, she realizes she has a ways to go before she gets the life she had planned. All of a sudden, Holly must change her plans and she finds herself flying by the seat of her pants (so to speak) yet again.

The Goal
Holly leaves New York and heads to South America
We can't say for sure whether Holly ever reaches her goal, in part because we don't always know what her goal really is. She does leave New York and escapes going to jail for her involvement with Sally Tomato, so in that way she has secured her freedom. But that might be the only way the novel completes this stage in Booker's plot since we don't get a clear sense of Holly's fate.

Three Act Plot Analysis

Act I
Holly and the narrator meet and become friends, and he then finds himself quickly entrenched in her chaotic life. When Holly decides to leave New York with José, there is no going back for her or the narrator since their relationship is forever changed.

Act II
Holly gets arrested for being involved with Sally Tomato, and the neat and tidy life in Brazil that she imagined for herself suddenly becomes farthest from her reach. Neither Holly nor the narrator (or us for that matter) knows what will happen to her.

Act III
José leaves Holly, she leaves New York, and the narrator gets a postcard from her from South America. He becomes a successful writer and moves out of the brownstone but we're not really sure what happens to her.

Study Questions

1. If you could write an alternate ending for the novel, what would it be and why?
2. How might our perception of Holly be different if the novel was told from her point of view?
3. Capote makes sure that we know that Holly is just nineteen years old. Why might this detail be important?
4. Why do you think the narrator remains unnamed?
5. Which detail of Holly's life do you particularly wish you knew more about? Why?
6. Capote breaks the novel up into short, quick chapters. How does that influence the way we read?
7. Which secondary character do you think is most important to the story. Why?

Characters

All Characters

Holly Golightly Character Analysis

Holly is one of those literary characters that academic folks love to talk about since she isn't as cut and dried as she initially appears. She might first seem like a party girl with no substance, who cares only about money and about finding the next fun thing, but if we spend a little time with her we see that there's a lot more there.

Holly was orphaned at a young age and we learn that her childhood was pretty rough since she was forced to move in with some pretty terrible relatives after her parents' deaths. She and her brother Fred eventually run away and they end up living at Doc Golightly's after one of his daughters finds them trying to steal milk. The two look so pitiful that Doc takes them in, and Holly eventually marries him because he's been so good to her and because, as she tells us, she loves him. And at some point it becomes clear that Holly develops real affection for the narrator. She also seems to care a good deal about Sally Tomato (even though he's paying her to hang out with him). So it's obvious that she does have emotional depth.

And we can't forget about her attachment to her brother Fred and her reaction when she finds out that he's been killed in action. Holly's rare but meaningful revelations about her brother show us that there was a happier period in her life, a time when she had her brother near to keep her warm. And they also show us that Holly's painful past is never far from her thoughts – Fred seems to be the one shining light in her otherwise difficult childhood, and memories of him probably also bring with them recollections of the less happy times he helped her deal with. Fred's absence while he's at war lets us know that Holly really has no one she completely trusts or feels comfortable around since Fred was always the one to provide that for her:

"Like my brother Fred. We used to sleep four in a bed, and he was the only one that ever let me hug him on a cold night." (3.7)

When Holly asks the narrator if she can call him Fred since he reminds her of her brother, we see that perhaps she's trying to recapture that safe and warm feeling she had with her brother.

So, what are we supposed to make of Holly Golightly? It's true that there's a lot for us to not like about her. She steals Mag's fiancée, she doesn't seem to care who she inconveniences in order to get what she wants or needs, most of her personal relationships seem fleeting and meaningless, and she never settles down the way we hope she might. Plus, although she does seem to develop genuine affection for the narrator, and although this relationship appears to matter to her, even that one is ultimately short-lived, too.

But there's also a lot to really like about Holly, and we might even feel sympathetic for her when we learn how she's ended up in New York fending for herself. Holly forces us as readers to question notions of who the good guy is and who the bad guy is. Are we supposed to like her? To despise her? To hope for a happy ending? To think that one day she has to pay for her carelessness? She doesn't make it easy for us to answer these questions, but we think this is what makes her such an interesting character. Holly's a bit of a challenge, and we have to appreciate her for that.

Holly Golightly Timeline and Summary

- Holly meets the narrator by climbing into his bedroom window one night.
- Holly throws loud and raucous parties, usually attended by lots of men. She invites the narrator to one of these parties and this is when we learn about her time in Hollywood from O.J. Berman.
- We also learn of her regular visits to Sally Tomato in Sing Sing prison. She does it for the money but also because she really likes the man.
- Holly and the narrator get into a wicked argument and avoid each other in the halls of the apartment building after the fight. But then Doc Golightly shows up to reclaim his wife, and this prompts her reconciliation with the narrator.
- Holly and Doc have a happy reunion and we find out that they sleep together. But she doesn't return to Texas with him and instead stays in New York.
- Holly, Rusty, Mag, and José go on a trip to Florida, during which Holly and José start having an affair. After they return, Holly finds out that Fred has been killed in action and she has a complete breakdown and destroys everything in her apartment. She never talks about Fred again.
- After Fred's death, Holly throws herself into domestic life with José and we find out that she's going to have a baby. Eventually, José proposes to Holly and she plans to go to Brazil with him.
- On one of her last days in New York, Holly invites the narrator to go horseback riding in Central Park. He almost gets into a terrible accident with his horse and Holly races to help him, and she's able to help stop his out-of-control horse.
- Later that evening, Holly gets arrested for her role in the drug ring run by Sally Tomato. She ends up in the hospital because she lost the baby after the horse fiasco with the

narrator. While she's in the hospital, she learns José has left her in order to avoid being associated with the scandal.

- She decides she's still going to go to Brazil since her ticket is already paid for, and she succeeds in leaving the country without being caught by authorities. The narrator doesn't hear from her for months, but she finally sends him a postcard from Buenos Aires. We learn that she has fallen in love with a married man and that she hasn't found a place to settle since she can't live with this guy. She promises to write to the narrator when she's more settled, but he never hears from her again and we're left to wonder what happens to Holly at the end of the novel.

The Narrator Character Analysis

Although we never learn the narrator's real name, he's still central to the novel, more for what he tells us about Holly than for what he tells us about himself. In fact, we actually learn very little about him throughout the story. We know that he's a writer, that he has moved to New York to pursue his career writing short stories, that he finds Holly's life very strange and different from his own, and that he eventually falls in love with her (although the nature of this love is never fully defined). But beyond that, he remains kind of a mystery to us.

We do get glimpses of his personality when he disagrees with Holly, when he feels hurt by the things she says and does, and when he experiences great sadness at the thought of losing her. However, this all comes to us in short bursts and we never really get inside the narrator's head. Why does he let her into his bedroom in the first place? What did he do before becoming a writer? What is his family like? We never get the answers to these types of questions, or even to more mundane ones. For example, when he tells us about his new job he offers little in the way of actual information:

"Because toward the end of the month I found a job: what is there to add? The less the better, except to say that it was necessary and lasted from nine to five." (8.1)

Who knows what he does all day every day? Not us, since he doesn't tell us.

The narrator functions more as a way for us to learn about Holly. It's through his eyes that we see her, through his descriptions that we get to know what happens to her throughout the course of the novel, and it's in his words that we read about her. In this way, we might consider the narrator less as a fully-developed character and more as an important literary device. He paints the picture of Holly Golightly for us, and without him we'd really have no story to read.

The Narrator Timeline and Summary

- The narrator meets Holly late one night after seeing her in the halls of the apartment building a few times before. She knocks on his bedroom window and he lets her into his

- apartment and into his life.
- The two start spending a lot of time together and the narrator comes to regard Holly as pretty important to him. When he doesn't get to see her, he misses her presence a great deal.
- Things seem to be going along fine until the narrator finds out that one of his stories is going to be published. When he races to her apartment to tell Holly about this exciting news, the two end up having a nasty argument since she totally misunderstands and then criticizes his writing. She throws him out of her apartment and he vows to never speak to her again.
- He keeps his promise for a while, but then he meets Doc Golightly, and when he subsequently learns more about Holly's childhood he feels a bit more inclined to forgive her.
- The neighbors resume their friendship, but then the narrator learns that Holly is planning to leave New York and move to Brazil with José. This throws him into deep sadness since he realizes that he's never been part of the plans she has for her life.
- Before she leaves, Holly takes the narrator horseback riding and the outing's a catastrophe. His horse freaks out after being scared by a group of boys and takes off running out of the park and onto Fifth Avenue. It's only after Holly and a policeman catch up to him that the narrator's horse stops, and in a cab on the way home he passes out from the shock.
- After Holly gets arrested and decides to leave the country, the narrator helps her get her stuff together, even though he's still devastated that she's leaving. On the way to the airport she drops her cat off in a strange neighborhood, for which the narrator roundly criticizes her. When she realizes the mistake she has made and unsuccessfully tries to find her cat, he promises to find the cat for her and to take care of it in her absence.
- He does eventually find the cat leading a seemingly happy life in a new home. We learn that he sells a few more stories and eventually moves out of the apartment building because it has too many memories of Holly. As the novel reaches its conclusion, the narrator gets the aforementioned postcard from Holly and we're left with his final thought: that he hopes she has found a place where she belongs.

Fred and Doc Golightly Character Analysis

Fred, Holly's brother, and Doc, the man who took her and Fred in as children and who she's married to, are pretty minor characters when it comes to actual action in the story (in fact, we never actually meet Fred and instead just hear about him from Holly). However, we think these two are important nonetheless because they both signify a time in Holly's life before she is the girl we know in New York. It's through Doc that we learn about Holly as a young girl, about the death of her parents, and about the hard life she's forced to lead when she no longer has her mom and dad around. And Holly's affection for the husband who's old enough to be her father shows us a rare glimpse of a sweeter, more sentimental young woman. Doc is one of our few links to Holly's past, and for this reason we think he's worth noting.

And speaking of Holly's past, perhaps no one is more important than Fred. We never meet him,

never hear directly from him, and Holly mentions him just a few times. But he is the one person she keeps consistently close to her heart, and the one person we can say without a doubt that she loves and worries about and whose feelings she actually takes into consideration. For most of the story, the life she could have with Fred after he returns from war is Holly's idea of happiness. We see her lose control just once in the story – when she hears of Fred's death. His profound impact on her is what makes this "minor" character not so minor after all. Like Doc, Fred is a vehicle through which we learn about our protagonist from someone other than the narrator, and like Doc, his presence in the story might make us like Holly just a little more. Consider this statement from Holly about the brother she loves so much:

"Everybody thought it was dotty, the way he gorged himself on peanut butter; he didn't care about anything in this world except horses and peanut butter. Be he wasn't dotty, just sweet and vague and terribly slow; he'd been in the eighth grade three years when I ran away. Poor Fred. I wonder if the Army's generous with their peanut butter." (3.22)

Holly has very little patience for most people's quirks, but she seems to love Fred all the more because of his. She remembers her sweet, not-too-bright brother and worries that he's not getting what he needs in the Army, and this description of her brother tells us a lot about her.

José Ybarra-Jaegar Character Analysis

Like most of the other characters in the novel, José is interesting because of what he can tell us about Holly. When Fred dies and Holly has to change her future plans, she seems to really enjoy acting as José's wife. She cooks for him, mends his clothes, and takes his suits to the cleaners. She also seems truly happy when she thinks she'll be moving to Brazil to start her family with him.

José's presence in Holly's life (and the stability he represents for her) reveals to us that perhaps her crazy life isn't as fulfilling as she wants everyone to believe. For a brief period of time, José offers Holly the chance to feel settled, to feel like she finally belongs somewhere, and to feel like she no longer has to go to Tiffany's when she's having the "mean reds." And when he leaves her because he's too much of a "coward" (17.8) to be associated with her after the arrest, she's truly sad because she really " *did* love him" (17.13). José is one of the rare characters in the novel who has an actual impact on Holly, who has the ability to both make her happy and to upset her, and we think this makes him quite worthy of consideration since so few people have this power.

Joe Bell Character Analysis

Joe's a pretty interesting guy in that he's kind of gruff and rough around the edges, but he's also a big softie when it comes to Holly and he offers her (dare we say it?) a sense of unconditional love. The novel opens with Joe and he reappears at the very end when Holly is preparing to leave New York. It's Joe who jumps into action when Holly gets arrested, Joe who worries about what will happen to her if she gets caught trying to leave the country, and even

Joe who arranges to have a limo take Holly to the airport even though he thinks she's making a huge mistake. And the final good-bye between Joe and Holly is one of the sweetest moments in the whole story. After surprising her with the limo, he struggles to hand her a bouquet of flowers or to look her in the eye:

"Kind, dear Mr. Bell. Look at me, sir." He wouldn't. He wrenched the flowers from the vase and thrust them at her; they missed their mark, scattered on the floor. "Good-bye," he said; and, as though he were going to vomit, scurried to the men's room. (18.9-18.10)

OK, the vomit part might not be that sweet (but it kind of is since it shows us how upset he is), but Joe sees something in Holly that compels him to love her no matter what she does, which makes him a pretty rare bird when it comes to the men in her life. He wants nothing from her, which we can't say for most of the other characters, and this makes us really, really like him.

Character Roles

Protagonist
Holly Golightly
The protagonist is really the central character of the story, and Holly is clearly at the center of everything that happens in *Breakfast at Tiffany's* . But she's kind of a complex one since the protagonist is usually considered the "good guy," and we might not all agree that Holly is so good. Do we like her all of the time? Probably not. Do we understand the choices she makes? Not really. But she's the link to all the other characters and it's her story that drives the narrative. Plus, there are things about her that are kind of endearing and, at some point, most of us probably do start to root for this complicated lady.

Antagonist
José Ybarra-Jaegar
There are several characters we could assign the "antagonist" role to, but we feel José is one of the most significant because of what he offers Holly and what he then takes away from her. When José proposes to Holly, who is pregnant with his child, he promises her a life of stability and security after Fred's death. But he doesn't love her enough to stick by her after she gets arrested, and he tells her so by writing a letter (he doesn't even have the guts to tell her face-to-face). José even thinks that Holly is still pregnant when he heads to Brazil without her, so he leaves his fiancée and what he thinks is their child to fend for themselves. José's departure robs Holly of the settled life she desires, and we think this makes him especially villainous. He tries to justify his decision to her and he humbly asks for her forgiveness, but that doesn't make him any more likable in our eyes. In the end he's still a guy who abandons the mother of his child.The narrator

Guide/Mentor
The Narrator
The narrator isn't really a guide in the spiritual sense, but he comes as close as possible to being a guide for readers as we navigate the events of Holly's life. He's the one who leads us

through her trials and tribulations, through her highs and lows, and he's the one who directs us from the very first page of the novel to the very last.

Foil
Holly and the Narrator
Although we know very little about the narrator, he and Holly are quintessential foils. Where Holly is impetuous and flighty, the narrator is careful and methodical. He seems to have lived a pretty sheltered life and she clearly has not. Their differences help characterize them as we're able to measure one against the other.

Character Clues

Names
Characters' names are pretty significant in the novel and they offer direct commentary on the personalities and qualities of the people they are attached to. Holly is perhaps our most blatant example of this. Her full name is Holiday Golightly, and this perfectly describes who she is and how she lives her life. Every day is a holiday for her and several critics have noted that "lightly" is precisely how she lives her life. She flits around from one good time to the next with little thought for any potential consequences and with little thought for the "heavy" things that might result from her actions.

Rusty's name is also representative of his character. His full name is Rusty Trawler, and a trawler is a large commercial ship. We know that Rusty has money (this speaks to the commercial part), but the "rusty" part is also interesting. Rust signifies something old and ignored, something that hasn't been taken care of, and something that has lost its luster and beauty. These all describe the character Rusty quite well.

Direct Characterization
Capote reveals a lot about his characters by simply telling us about them. Take a look at the passage in which the narrator first sees Holly:

"She was still on the stairs, now she reached the landing, and the ragbag colors of her boy's hair, tawny streaks, strands of albino-blond and yellow, caught the hall light. It was a warm evening, nearly summer, and she wore a slim cool black dress, black sandals, a pearl choker. For all her chic thinness, she had an almost breakfast-cereal air of health, a soap and lemon cleanness, a rough pink darkening in the cheeks." (2.12)

This is the most detailed description of Holly we get in the entire novel, and it comes to us by way of the narrator simply telling us about her with the attention of a writer.

Actions
We learn a lot about the characters by what they do. Holly continues to steal even though she no longer has to, just to stay in practice. This tells us that at some point she had to go to some pretty drastic measures just to survive and that she worries that she might still have to some day. Joe Bell orders a limo for Holly even though he doesn't want her to leave, which reveals

what a big heart he has under his gruff exterior. And the narrator keeps his promise to find Holly's cat, showing us how truly loyal he is. The things these characters do tell us a great deal about who they are.

Literary Devices

Symbols, Imagery, Allegory

Holly's Cat

Holly's cat is a constant reminder of the lack of connection she feels to those around her. For much of the story, he represents her unwillingness (or maybe her inability) to feel tied down to anyone or anything, and the fact that she won't name him further emphasizes this: "We just sort of took up by the river one day, we don't belong to each other: he's an independent, and so am I" (4.52). Holly won't claim the cat as her own because that would signify that she's putting down roots, and this is something she's clearly adverse to doing.

Near the end of the story, the cat comes to represent something slightly different. Holly sets him free on her way to the airport, but she does so by leaving him in an unfamiliar and unfriendly-looking neighborhood. When she realizes the horrible mistake she has made and tries desperately to find him, the cat symbolizes Holly's realization that she's scared about never belonging anywhere or to anyone. All of her fears come to rest in the symbol of the cat, and the fact that she doesn't find him might tell us something about her eventual fate.

Holly's Sunglasses/Masks

Holly is rarely without her dark glasses, and these quite obviously prevent people from seeing what's going on behind them. Her eyes are almost always covered up, making it difficult to know what she's feeling at any given moment (you know, the whole "eyes are the window to the soul" thing). The dark glasses represent yet another way for Holly to keep those around her from getting too close and the shades are a physical and literal way for her to cover herself up, to prevent herself from being exposed. They serve, in many ways, as a mask.

Other masks appear in the story as well, particularly in the scene when Holly and the narrator steal Halloween masks from a drugstore. They wear the stolen masks all the way home, again concealing their true identities from each other and from the world around them. The novel is filled with people hiding behind something, and for Holly it's often something as obvious as a mask.

Birdcage

Holly gives the narrator an antique birdcage for Christmas, but she doesn't like what it means one bit. She appreciates "its fantasy" (7.4), but she cannot "bear to see anything in a cage" (7.1), and it doesn't take much digging to figure out why. Holly never wants to feel caged in herself, never wants to feel like she can't just pick and go when the mood strikes her, and the birdcage represents the confinement she fights so hard against. It might be beautiful and momentarily desirable to her, but in the end it still functions as a way to keep whatever's inside

it from being free, and this is an idea Holly simply can't get behind.

Tiffany's

The jewelry store is Holly's escape; it's the place she can go where she feels entirely safe from the "mean reds" that plague her from time to time. Tiffany's is a refuge Holly, and it represents order and security and stability to her. She wants to find a place in the world that she can claim as her own, and she knows that such a place will feel like Tiffany's to her. Tiffany's symbolizes all that the outside world is not, and Holly holds onto it as her ideal.

Setting

New York City during World War II

Breakfast at Tiffany's is set in New York during World War II. The war doesn't figure prominently in the story in that we don't see the main characters in combat and most of them seem untouched by the realities of war. But the specter of war sort of hovers throughout the novel as we hear about rationing things like peanut butter, we learn that most apartments lack of telephones during this time, and most devastatingly, we are told about the loss of Holly's brother Fred who dies while serving as a soldier.

The city of New York figures pretty prominently in the story. Holly loves the city, loves the Brooklyn Bridge, loves the "lights, the river" (12.4), and she vows to return with her kids so they can see the things she loves. New York offers an exciting background to the story and it lends the narrative a definite energy. It's hard to imagine the story of Holly Golightly happening anywhere else.

Much of the action takes place in or around an old brownstone apartment building where both Holly and the narrator live. It's here that the narrator first meets Holly, here that they develop their friendship, and here that most of the major events occur (Holly learns of Fred's death in her apartment, she gets arrested in the narrator's apartment, she's reunited with Doc in the building, and she and the narrator have their first argument there). It's like a little world with its own good times and bad times, its own conflicts and eccentric characters, and its own memories (the narrator has to move after Holly leaves because the building starts to feel "haunted" (19.1).

Holly's apartment is also its own special place. It's little and messy and noisy and it tells us a lot about her character. She doesn't bother to furnish her abode (except for the bedroom, but just a little bit), which adds to the general sense of impermanence that surrounds her (take a look at the "Themes" section in this guide for more on this). It suits Holly and it becomes an exciting destination for the narrator, who never knows who or what he'll find there.

So the setting is a mixture of all of these elements. It's the war and New York and the brownstone apartment building. And it's Holly's apartment and the things this space represents for the various characters.

Narrator Point of View

First Person (Central Narrator)

Breakfast at Tiffany's is told in the first person from the point of view of an unnamed narrator. And the narrator in this story is interesting since he is telling us his story but, in the end, the novel is mostly about Holly. In this respect, he would seem to operate as a third person narrator, since in many ways he's telling us someone else's story while relating his own. But the novel is framed around the narrator's experience in New York, his experiences with Holly, and his telling of the events that occur (which is what makes this first person). There are definite advantages to this since Holly would probably be an unreliable narrator of her own life. And since so much of Holly's character depends on her interaction with other people, it seems only fitting that we get to know her through the eyes of someone who has the good luck (or misfortune depending on which camp you fall in) to know her.

There are disadvantages (or at least complications) associated with a first person narrator, though. We only directly get the unnamed narrator's view of Holly and of the events that occur, and he's clearly emotionally involved in what's going on, so we should probably question how accurate his recollections are. His views of Holly are probably very different from Fred's or Doc Golightly's or Joe Bell's, but because we have a single point of view, we don't get to know these other perceptions. And since he can't be with Holly every hour of every day, and since we know that she isn't very forthcoming with truly personal details about herself, there's a lot we probably don't get to know just because we're not in her head.

This isn't to say that Capote made a bad choice or that one type of narrator is better than another, but it does allow us to question what we gain and what we lose with a first person narrator, especially when that narrator is not the central character of the story.

Genre

Literary Fiction

As a genre, literary fiction depends a lot on characters, and there's no denying that Holly is pretty central to *Breakfast at Tiffany's* . It's true that a lot happens in the story, and the events that occur certainly are exciting and salacious and necessary to the narrative. Holly's pregnancy, her arrest, the affair with José, the story about her time in Hollywood, and even the narrator's disastrous horseback ride in Central Park all drive the story. But, in the end, we think these dramatic elements all reflect attempts to reveal Holly's character to us. Each thing that happens results in a fuller picture of who Holly is, and in this way the plot serves to create character depth. In the end, the novel is a study of Holly Golightly, and that's why we think it qualifies as literary fiction.

Tone

Sympathetic, Emotionally-involved

This might sound a little complicated, but Capote's attitude toward Holly can be different than our reactions to her (and we think this is part of his talent). Some of us might not like her or feel any sympathy for her, but Capote seems to do both. He actually presents us with a lot of reasons to dislike Holly, but he's also careful to temper that with some information that probably elicits a sympathetic reaction to other parts of her life. For example, after she coldly criticizes the narrator's writing without any thought of how her words might hurt his feelings, we're soon introduced to Doc and he tells us the sad story of Holly and Fred's childhood:

"Well, you never saw a more pitiful something. Ribs sticking out everywhere, legs so puny they can't hardly stand, teeth wobbling so bad they can't chew mush. Story was: their mother died of the TB, and their papa done the same – and all the churren, a whole raft of 'em, they been sent off to live with different mean people. Now Lulamae and her brother, them two been living with some mean, no-count people a hundred miles east of Tulip. She had good cause to run off from that house." (9.18)

No matter what we might think of Holly as an adult (and some of us might use the term "adult" loosely when discussing her), it's pretty hard not to feel bad for a young child with no parents, who has no food to eat and no safe place to live. Capote doesn't gloss over her negative qualities, but he does present us with details that complicate these downfalls. We get a better idea of why she does whatever she must to survive, and there are enough of these types of details in the novel to suggest that Capote himself feels a good deal of sympathy for her as opposed to a desire to criticize his novel's heroine.

Writing Style

Direct, Straightforward

Capote isn't afraid to be blunt, and he doesn't shy away from using language that many readers might find shocking or offensive. But since so much of the writing in the novel is dialogue from Holly, this seems only fitting she sure isn't afraid to be blunt either. Let's take a look at a passage in which Holly discusses wanting a roommate who is a lesbian:

"Incidentally," she said, "do you happen to know *any nice lesbians? I'm looking for a roommate. Well, don't laugh. I'm so disorganized, I simply can't afford a maid; and really, dykes are wonderful home-makers, they love to do all the work, you never have to bother about brooms and defrosting and sending out the laundry."* (3.31)

Holly throws around some incredibly derogatory language here and she resorts to huge generalizations about people based on sexual preference. Yet we have to remember that writing style is one of the tools an author has at his or her disposal to help create a character, and this passage seems quintessentially Holly to us. We might cringe at some of her words, but

we also have to recognize this as Capote being totally in tune with the character he's created.

What's Up With the Title?

Although Holly actually mentions Tiffany's (and having breakfast there) just a few times in the short novel, we think her reference to it is a pretty important element of the text, and it tells us a lot about her character. It's true that Tiffany's is expensive and that the things in it are out of her reach (at least for the time being), but it's the *idea* of Tiffany's and the perfection that Holly associates with the store and the brand that makes her feel better when she's scared or sad or angry. It's the belief that only good things happen there that makes Tiffany's so appealing to her.

So why choose this as the title? Well, there are several possibilities. The title draws attention to Holly without having to name her specifically – she's the only one in the book who loves the store so much. And since the novel takes place during World War II, when people were forced to ration everything from food to gasoline, there's something really pleasant about the thought of eating a meal in the middle of an opulent, shiny store that seems untouched by all the crazy things that are happening otherwise. And the title *sounds* like one for a novel that would be about light and fluffy stuff, which it really isn't, which we think this makes for a pretty cool title. It can do so much and mean so much, all while sounding like it's pretty insignificant.

What's Up With the Ending?

There isn't a lot we can say for certain about the ending of the novel, but isn't that what makes it worth thinking about? We do know that Holly has ended up in Argentina (at least according to her postcard), we know that the narrator is finally able to locate Holly's cat, and we know that he wishes good things for Holly in the end. But what we don't know for sure is if we're left with a happy ending or if Holly's life is just going to continue to be as crazy and as chaotic as it has been for the rest of the novel. After all, we as readers may find the story of her life interesting and a little exotic since it's probably so unlike our own lives. But at some point it becomes pretty clear that Holly's life scares her a little bit, and if we like her at all this might make us feel bad for her. So it's hard to know what to make of the ending, but this is OK since this allows us to come up with our own interpretations.

On the one hand, Holly seems like she's found happiness in Buenos Aires. She's escaped going to jail for being associated with Sally Tomato, she's fallen in love with a " *duhvine $enor*" (19.1) as she tells us in her postcard to the narrator (we're guessing the "$" in his name means he's divine *and* divinely rich), and she seems to be living the same kind of exciting life she had in New York. So, this all sounds pretty good for her, and this is certainly one of the many ways we can interpret the ending.

But it's also possible that the ending is not as happy as it seems. Holly also tells us that the man she's fallen in love with is married and has kids, and that she has no place to live because she can't live with him. So she's ended up with yet another unavailable man and is still moving around, not really belonging anywhere, as a result. And when the narrator tells us that he never hears from Holly after this postcard, we're left to wonder what actually happens to her. Maybe

she's blissfully happy for the rest of her life, but maybe she's still scared of never finding a place to call her own, never forging long-lasting, meaningful relationships with anyone, and never feeling settled. We don't really know what happens to Holly Golightly, so we're left wondering with the narrator if she ever finds a place where she belongs.

This open-endedness might bug some of us since it's often easier to deal with a text that actually provides some clear closure to the events in the novel, and *Breakfast at Tiffany's* doesn't do this. But we think the texts that *don't* sum everything up for us cab be even more fun since we get the chance to create a little meaning ourselves. Regardless of your stance there, the open ending is pretty cool in that it reflects Holly's character in a lot of ways. Holly is all over the place and is hard to read and difficult to understand, but something in the narrator and in readers wants to keep trying. The ending of the novel is kind of the same. Plus, Capote does something pretty cool by creating a circular structure with the ending that links back to the beginning of the novel. Remember that Joe and the narrator don't know where Holly is or what she's been up to when we first start reading, and even after all we go through with her throughout the course of the novel, we *still* don't know where she is or what she's up to by the end. In this way, the open-ended conclusion seems kind of perfect.

Did You Know?

Trivia

- Truman Capote's given name was Truman Streckfus Persons. Capote was his stepfather's last name. (Source)
- Capote was originally going to name Holly's character Connie Gustafson. (Source)
- A woman named Bonnie Golightly sued Capote for $800,000, "charging invasion of privacy as well as libel" (314). (Source: Clarke, Gerald. *Capote: A Biography.* New York: Carroll & Graff, 1988)
- *Harper's Bazaar* was going to publish *Breakfast at Tiffany's* , but when Capote refused to get rid of the bad language or to change Holly's occupation, the magazine pulled the novel. (Source)

Steaminess Rating

R
There isn't any explicit sex in *Breakfast at Tiffany's* , but we do get some frank sexual talk. Holly tells the narrator that she has sex with Doc before he heads back to Texas, we know that she has had eleven lovers (not counting the ones before she was thirteen years old), and she's very open in her discussion of homosexuality. She throws around some un-PC epithets about gay women that might be a little shocking to some readers, and this ups the sex rating a little. But we never get firsthand accounts of people actually doing the deed.

Allusions and Cultural References

Literary and Philosophical References

- William Saroyan (3.14)
- Ernest Hemingway (3.14)
- W. Somerset Maugham (3.16)
- Emily Brontë, *Wuthering Heights* (8.20)

Historical References

- Sigmund Freud (4.16)
- Unity Mitford, a supporter and friend of Hitler's (4.41)
- Adolf Hitler (4.41)
- Cleopatra (6.6)
- Nero, Roman emperor (12.2)
- Nehru, prime minister of India from 1947-1964 (12.3)
- Wendell Wilkie, Republican nominee in the 1940 presidential election (12.3)

Pop Culture References

- Gilbert and Sullivan, nineteenth-century composers (1.4)
- Our Gal Sunday, radio soap (1.4)
- Cole Porter and Kurt Weill (3.5)
- *Oklahoma!* (3.5)
- Luise Rainer, German film actress (4.18)
- *The Story of Dr. Wassell*, 1944 Cecil B. DeMille film (4.20)
- Cecil B. DeMille, film director (4.20)
- David O. Selznick, producer (4.34)
- William Randolph Hearst (12.2)
- Bergdorf, upscale New York department store (3.41)
- "21," famous club/restaurant (3.3)
- Tiffany's (4.51)

Biblical References

- St. Christopher (8.10)

Best of the Web

Websites

Paris Review Interview with Capote

http://www.theparisreview.org/viewinterview.php/prmMID/4867

This is a great interview in which Capote discusses his childhood, his literary influences, his writing habits, and his hobbies.

American Masters Biography of Capote

http://www.pbs.org/wnet/americanmasters/episodes/truman-capote/about-the-author/58/

A brief PBS biography that covers Capote's life and career.

Lyrics to "Moon River"

http://www.reelclassics.com/Movies/Tiffanys/moonriver-lyrics.htm

Visit this link to read the lyrics of Henry Mancini's award-winning theme song for the 1961 movie. The site also has a link to an audio recording of the song.

Capote Times Topics Page

http://topics.nytimes.com/topics/reference/timestopics/people/c/truman_capote/index.html

The *New York Times*'s page on Capote, which links to tons of great articles about the author and his works.

Movie or TV Productions

Breakfast at Tiffany's , 1961

http://www.imdb.com/title/tt0054698/

The famous film starring Audrey Hepburn as Holly Golightly.

Video

Audrey Hepburn Singing "Moon River"

http://www.youtube.com/watch?v=BOByH_iOn88

This is a clip of Hepburn as Holly Golightly in the film adaptation of the novel.

Images

Photograph of Truman Capote

http://tuvoisceque.canalblog.com/images/h_cartier_bresson._Truman_Capote_1947.jpg

Check out this photo of a young Capote in 1947.

Audrey Hepburn as Holly Golightly

http://scoop.diamondgalleries.com/public/news_images/4/77628_189093_4.jpg

This is an iconic image of Hepburn, which was taken during the filming of the movie.

Printed in Great Britain by
Amazon.co.uk, Ltd.,
Marston Gate.